TAO

PHILIP RAWSON
and LASZLO LEGEZA

TAO

The Chinese philosophy of time and change

with 196 illustrations, 33 in color

THAMES AND HUDSON

ART AND IMAGINATION
General Editor: Jill Purce

Published in the USA in 1979 by
Thames and Hudson Inc., 500 Fifth Avenue,
New York, New York 10110

Reprinted 1991

Library of Congress Catalog Card Number
78-63580

Printed and bound in Singapore by
C.S. Graphics Pte Ltd.

Contents

ACKNOWLEDGMENTS
Objects in the plates are reproduced by courtesy of the following:

Barlow Collection, University of Sussex 20
Bowes Museum, Barnard Castle, Co. Durham 7
British Museum 24, 33
Freer Gallery of Art, Washington DC (courtesy of the Smithsonian Institution) 35, 36
Gulbenkian Museum of Oriental Art, Durham 1, 3, 8, 10, 11, 12, 13, 14, 17, 25, 27, 28, 29, 31, 47, 49, 50, 52, 55, 61, 62, 63
C. T. Loo Collection, Paris 38, 45
Museum of Fine Arts, Boston 40; 56, 57 (Francis Gardner Curtis Fund)
National Palace Museum, Taipei, Taiwan, Republic of China 44
Nelson Gallery, Kansas City 41
Percival David Foundation, London University 64
Private collections 32, 37, 48, 51, 53, 58, 59, 65
Roger Peyrefitte Collection, Paris 39
Royal Ontario Museum, Toronto 34
Royal Scottish Museum, Edinburgh 54
Shanghai Museum 19, 26, 42, 67
University Library, Durham 9
Victoria and Albert Museum, London 2, 15, 43, 46, 60, 66

Photographic credits collections as above except for the following:
Jeff Teasdale, Durham 1, 3, 7–14, 17–18, 20–3, 25, 27–32, 37, 42, 47–9, 51–3, 55, 58–9, 61–3, 65; *all documentary ills. except* 3, 8, 14, 16–17, 23, 25, 27, 32, 37, 45–6, 59, 63, 67, 82, 86, 100, 103, 107–8, 115–16, 121, 126 (museum photos) and those credited below
Eileen Tweedy *documentary ills.* 1, 4, 8, 28, 122–3
John Webb (Brompton Studios) *documentary ill.* 5

Introduction

THOUSANDS OF PEOPLE nowadays know about the yin and yang as Chinese male and female sexual energies. Perhaps they use the *I-ching*, or Book of Changes, the ancient Chinese oracle text, without understanding how it is meant to work. They may not realize that Chinese art expresses the same sense of the mystery and coherence of the world as the *I-ching*. Taoism is the key; and art can give us perhaps the most direct approach to the strange universe of fluid energies which Taoism manipulated with its sexual and yogic practices.

Life in China has always been appallingly dangerous, punctuated by episodes of uncontrollable and capricious violence. Invasions and rebellions repeatedly shattered whole provinces; massacres were common. In the country famine and flood were constant visitors. Forced military service repeatedly reduced the people to starvation. In the cities the powerful oppressed the less powerful; feuds resulted in entire families being murdered or destroyed, wives and children seized and enslaved. Legal punishments were hideous. Vicious intrigue and injustice surrounded the Imperial throne, for which merciless struggles were the rule. Even official life was dangerous for civil servants. One of China's greatest historians, for example, the official Ssu-ma Ch'ien (145–90(?) BC), was castrated for writing an accurate but unwelcome memorandum. Such was the turbulent sea in which the Chinese had to swim. It is not surprising that many became hermits, and that the Taoist 'mountain man', wrapped in outer and inner peace, communing with nature and dwelling in a personal paradise, became an ideal figure on to whom eighty generations projected their fantasies.

Everyone interested in art knows that the Chinese have one of the world's greatest and longest artistic traditions. Its treasures have been collected and imitated for centuries in the West. Our notions of aesthetic quality owe much to China. But despite this long interest, Western appreciation of Chinese art has never got to the heart of the matter, and very few people have learned to see in Chinese art what the Chinese themselves put into it. So this book is meant to show Chinese art in a completely new light.

Most Western collectors content themselves with admiring in a general way the technical finesse and atmosphere of Chinese pictures, or the qualities of shape, glaze and texture of ceramics; and arranging them in chronological order. They never realize that each object they so much admire spoke a language for its Chinese makers which conveyed a clear, non-verbal meaning; and that the object was meant to make people who used it aware of their own environment in a special, and to us unfamiliar, way. It was supposed, quite literally, to work a transformation on the world and open the users' minds to their own intimate relationship with their universe. A good work of art should be an embodiment of – and a pointer to – the Tao.

This word Tao has no single correct translation. Its meaning goes beyond words, even in Chinese. The great Chinese texts devoted to it – especially the *Tao-te-ching* and the *Chuang-tzu* – are collections of sayings, stories and allegories which point at its meaning from different directions. And many passages are themselves so ambiguous as to defy translation. This may partly be due to accidents of history and confusions which have crept into the texts; but the Chinese have come to accept it as a vital feature. For, like so much in Chinese culture, especially art, these passages mean not one thing alone, but several things at once; none contains the whole meaning on its own. Even in China the word Tao has been used by different groups of philosophers in different ways. But these special usages are really limitations imposed on a fundamental notion which is far wider than they, being deeply rooted in the Chinese mind, with its customs, languages and unspoken assumptions, and can easily embrace them all.

> Vast indeed is the Ultimate Tao,
> Spontaneously itself, apparently without acting,
> End of all ages and beginning of all ages,
> Existing before Earth and existing before Heaven,
> Silently embracing the whole of time,
> Continuing uninterrupted through all eons,
> In the East it taught Father Confucius,
> In the West it converted the 'Golden man' [the Buddha]
> Taken as pattern by a hundred kings,
> Transmitted by generations of sages,
> It is the ancestor of all doctrines,
> The mystery beyond all mysteries.

This quotation is from a Ming rock inscription dated Spring 1556. It demonstrates that Confucians, Buddhists, Mohists, as well as Taoists, who all use the term Tao in their own ways to indicate their chief principle, are talking, for all their differences, about fundamentally the same thing. In this century Mao Tse-tung *(plate 30)* has, in *his* own way, developed a political version of the intrinsically Chinese Tao.

There have been many schools and cults which call themselves officially Taoist. They flourished at different times in various parts of China, and generated many variant doctrines; often they have been persecuted as non-conformists. They produced a vast literature that no Westerner, and probably no Oriental, has ever read entire. The *Tao-tsang* is a Ming printed collection of these (AD 1445), and contains 1,464 individual works. Western academics sometimes busy themselves about distinguishing artists according to outer categories, Buddhist, Confucian or avowedly Taoist. In practice the distinctions are of marginal significance only. Certainly some Buddhist artists did some things which could not possibly be called Taoist, and their thought embodied a personal compassion which was foreign to Taoist thought; so, too, did early Confucian painters. But by the Sung dynasty (960–1279) the modes of expression used by mainstream artists, whatever their religion, had blended. All shared a common attitude to the world and to art; their lives were ordered by the same rituals, which were in turn governed by Imperial edicts issued from the heart of the Empire; they shared the same literary inheritance, and knew the same classic texts. Many of the leading artists made a special point of knowing and combining all the doctrines in their own work. So it is true to say that each artist, in his own particular way, was illuminating another aspect of the infinite multiplicity of the Tao.

But perhaps most important of all is the fact that, although it lacked an organized 'Church', Taoism was the cult of the masses of the people. Whatever the ruling classes might do or think, the Chinese population was indelibly Taoist. Its culture revolved about divination, magic, medicine and the everyday ceremonies of life. It imagined star gods *(plate 1)*, mysterious Immortals, heavenly palaces just like earthly ones, glorious paradises and various kinds of supernatural rewards and punishments. While dynasties rose and fell the people preserved the essence. The 'Ancient Customs' of Taoism provided a permanent background to all Chinese art and thought. Let us go at once to the heart of the matter.

The Taoist perception of the real world differs essentially from our usual Western one. We tend to think, diagrammatically, of a world of separate things – some of them alive – arranged in an independent space. We take it for granted that these lumps of independent 'thing' 'cause' each other, 'act on' each other as they 'move about' in empty space, and pass through a series of static states of change. Even our philosophy and science limit themselves to finding substantial 'things', carefully divided from one another by definition, which will 'explain' the real world. Idealism calls them ideas, materialism calls them atoms, with their sub-atomic particles. We act on the assumption that our world is a structure assembled of solid building-bricks in many different shapes and sizes, all quite independent of the observer; each concept which denotes one of these building-bricks, its connection with others, or its activities, we take to exclude for ever its opposite or its own negative. The shapes of the building-bricks are fixed, mutually exclusive, and, by implication, unchangeable. Change happens, we assume, by one 'thing' turning into 'something else'. The way we experience and measure time is by dividing it up into countable moments, each of which is separate and, in an abstract way, identical to all others, however large or infinitely small we may choose to make them.

Taoism sees all this as schematic, vulgar and absurd. It recognizes that, though fixed concepts referring to things and states can be extracted by human thought from the mobile reality, and can be useful, there is actually no way of reconstructing the mobility of the real by adding up fixed concepts. Therefore, the most important element – the only element that matters – is always left out of the ordinary ideas most of us have, on which we base our worlds and with which we try to come to terms with them. All static conceptualism is in the last resort impotent. For even our most sophisticated cosmological reasoning arises from, and leads back to, integral concepts which have this enormous primary fallacy built into them. The Tao which Taoism knows, and with which its art is concerned, is a seamless web of unbroken movement and change, filled with undulations, waves, patterns of ripples and temporary 'standing waves' like a river *(plates 2–5)*. Every observer is himself an integral function of this web. It never stops, never turns back on itself, and none of its patterns of which we can take conceptual snapshots are real in the sense of being permanent, even for the briefest moment of time we can imagine. Like streaming clouds the objects and facts of our world are to the Taoist simply shapes and phases which last long enough in one general form for us to consider them as units *(plate 6)*. In a strong wind clouds change their shapes fast. In the slowest of the winds of Tao the mountains and rocks of the earth change their shapes very slowly – but continuously and certainly. Men simply find it hard to observe the fact.

All the separations which men claim to decipher in the web of Tao are useful fabrications, concepts being themselves ripples in the 'mental' part of the stream. Each human being himself is woven out of a complex system of totally mobile interactions with his environment. His body is in perpetual change, not by jumps from state to state; for his aging does not correspond to minutes, hours and birthdays, but goes on all the time. The reader of these words is not the same person who began to read this paragraph. It is only useful convention which justifies even our seeing a man, a tree, a rock, as a 'thing', instead of as a set of surfaces, each of which represents changes and transformations as they go on, some being visible 'outside', some invisible 'inside'. If the Westerner

1 *Tao*

imagines that the conceptual snapshots he takes of what is happening capture it in any but the most inadequate way, he is deluded. To realize this truth makes many Westerners very uncomfortable, and can inhibit them in coming to terms with Taoist art. It is also a fact that in China itself certain neo-Confucian philosophers, feeling a similar discomfort, and being anxious to preserve their sense of social and theoretical order, attempted to introduce some fixed elements into the Tao; these they called 'Li', principle, or shape and form.

Two of the most important aspects of the intuition of the Tao are, first; that nothing which happens, no event or process, ever repeats itself exactly. On the ordinary human scale this is obvious, if one stops to think. Only on the microscopic scale, where invisible sub-atomic particles are isolated as 'snapshot' concepts, may they seem to repeat. But, in fact, the overall context of even such minute apparent repetitions has changed while they were happening; their nature is anyway 'vibration'. Second; this immense web consisting of rolling change does not itself change. It is the 'uncarved block' devoid of any definable shape, the 'mother', matrix of time, including both 'being' and 'not being', the present, future and vanished past – the Great Whole of continuous duration, infinite space and infinite change.

In art the most powerful and common image for this Tao is the convoluted stone, full of holes and hollows eroded by water, whose shapes never repeat themselves *(plates 43, 47)*. Real stones with genuine Tao quality were eagerly sought by Chinese collectors. Big ones were dug out at the edges of lakes and rivers. Some of the best came, during T'ang and Sung times, from the Hsiao-hsia bay of T'ai-hu lake, and were the most expensive single objects in the Empire. The Imperial palace gardens were filled with them. Smaller ones were collected by scholars, mystics and artists; the great Sung painter Mi Fu was a passionate collector. Some looked like landscapes of mountains and valleys. Other kinds of stone were collected for the sake of their internal markings; but these have another meaning which will be discussed later. The twisted and eroded stone was a motif repeated tens of thousands of times in paintings and on ceramics, often combined with trees, flowers and birds. Its reference always is to this truth of Tao as a reality whose essence is never ceasing, perpetual, seamless process.

In the face of this intuition, what can man do? There is a relevant story told in the *Chuang-tzu*, one of the most revered Taoist books. One day Confucius and his pupils were walking by a turbulent river, which swept over rocks, rapids and waterfalls. They saw an old man swimming in the river, far upstream. He was playing in the raging water and went under. Confucius sent his pupils running downstream to try and save him. However, the old man beached safely on the bank, and stood up unharmed, the water streaming from his hair. The pupils brought him to Confucius, who asked him how on earth he had managed to survive in the torrent among the rocks. He answered, 'Oh, I know how to go in with a descending vortex, and come out with an ascending one.' He was, of course, a man of Tao.

The point of the story is that the Tao, that web of time and change, is a network of vortices like a moving and dangerous torrent of water; and the ideal Taoist is he who has learned to use all his senses and faculties to intuit the shapes of the currents in the Tao, so as to harmonize himself with them completely. Works of art provide some of the means for bringing people into communion with the currents and vortices, giving them a deep sense of their presence, and of the ways in which the tangled skeins evolve.

The works are meant actually to nourish or feed the inner man with matching energies. All true Taoist art is therefore a projection of time, of complex process, not of static conceptual shape. It is also, like Taoist literature, full of suggestions and hints at extra layers of meaning, which may not be obvious at first.

But if one is to be able to convey any idea of time at all one must have some basic units of thought and imagination, which can be developed as form in artistic terms. In Taoist art the two chief groups of imaginative unit are first: cyclic patterns of process; and second; linear threads or veins. The obvious examples of these are, first: the tri-grams of the *I-ching* oracle book, with their seasonal and directional significance; and second: the continuous mobile brush-line in painting. Both of these groups will be explained in a moment, with the various ways they are conceived and explored.

Before this, though, the most familiar and important elements of Taoist process need discussing: the mutual opposites called yin and yang. This pair is often misrepresented, especially in books on Chinese sexual theory, where yin is taken just to symbolize the female sexual energy and yang the male. In fact these two, like so much in Taoism, are almost infinitely ambiguous; for there exists no yang without yin in it, nor yin with-out yang. They are impalpable polarities which provide that oscillation without which there can be no movement. Their endless dialectic in vibration and wave-pattern is what weaves the web of the Tao. Yang is bright, red, male, penetrating, high, celestial. Yin is dark, black, female, receptive, abyssal, deep. Each is referred to by many symbols, used again and again in art. Their different combinations match different contexts. In stallion, dragon *(plates 10, 12)*, brilliant Feng-bird *(plate 43)*, ram *(plate 25)*, cock, horned beasts, jade, mountain *(plate 1)*, summer and the south – to name but a few – yang predominates. In fungus *(plate 8)*, whirling shapes of cloud and water *(plate 9)*, valley, winter, north, vase, peach, female dragon with divided tail, peony, fish and chrysanthemum, yin predominates.

All of these objects belong to the vocabulary of the secret Taoist language used everywhere in Chinese art; its symbols and allusions can be understood by those who know how to read them. Even in the actual execution of drawn shapes the dialectic can be seen at work. In landscape-painting the 'opening and closing' relationship of hills and valleys reveals it *(plate 41)*, as well as the combination of mountain and valley; among the actual strokes so do strong verticals *(plate 19)*, horizontals, concavities and bridge-forms. Paired colours, such as red and blue *(plate 20)*, red and green *(plates 29–30)*, white and blue or black, gold and silver, may carry the same dialectic significance. More subtle still, the complex, subdued colours used for the glazes of Sung ceramics – on Ju, Celadon or Kuan wares, for example – were deliberately intended as a reconciliation and harmonization of colour polarities.

For in Taoist art, as in Taoist life with its yoga, the aim is harmony: harmony be-tween the components of the dialectic situation, leading to harmony between each man and his turbulent universe, and an ultimate tranquillity. But harmony is impossible without 'forces' to harmonize, and of little value unless those forces are themselves at high power. So Taoist Chinese art is full of emblems of aroused yang and yin, com-bined so as to balance each other. It was Taoist theory that things brought into contact with each other, or arranged together, influenced each other. So works of art were made and used as practical magic. Their portrayals of harmony were meant to *induce* harmony. Potent designs appear on clothes, on the fine ritual vessels, bronze or ceramic, used on public or domestic altars for the sacrificial offerings which were daily duty among the Chinese. They were painted or carved on domestic pottery, and on the things used on the scholar's desk. The harmonic combinations might be, for example, a gorgeously plumed Feng-bird flying down into a garden of peony flowers *(plate 43)*; a dragon among swirling clouds *(plate 12)*; a woman with a ram *(plate 25)*; a colour combination of red and blue ceramic glazes melting together *(plate 20)*. Sometimes porcelain meant to be used in the women's apartments of a well-to-do household would have a strong bias towards yin in its ornament – such as the goddess Lan Ts'ai-ho *(plate 11)* or her flower-basket. This may have been for the express purpose of increasing the yin of the women who used it – for sexual reasons, as will appear later. In practice, too, each of these symbols will have other overtones of meaning which one can only discover by degrees.

There are other dialectic symbols which polarize and reconcile the functions of yang and yin. Such are Heaven and Earth, with 'Man' being located between them *(plate 14)*. This idea is probably the most important nuclear idea in the whole of Chinese culture. For all the problems of mankind, social, political, personal and religious, are seen in terms of reconciling the claims of Heaven and Earth. The emperor of China's chief role was as intermediary between the two, co-ordinating and harmonizing Heaven's impulses. Heaven symbolized the remote source of the multiplied energies working through the inert earth, where man laboured to perform favourable changes for himself, and in which he was buried. There is an extraordinary range of themes and motifs reflecting this conception. Dragons, so common in art, were the chief embodiments of such energies. And since the role of the emperor was to mediate between the two, co-ordinating and harmonizing Heaven's impulses upon the Earth, the dragon was the embodiment of Imperial power, and hence the Imperial emblem. It was blazoned on robes, jades, porcelain *(plate 60)*, architecture – always with this significance, as the celestial mobile energy whose body combined the attributes of goat, fish, lizard and deer.

Two basic emblematic shapes are the circle, for Heaven, and the square, for Earth *(plate 14)*. The shape of the ordinary Chinese cash-coin is a circle pierced by a square hole at the centre, with the inscription between the circle and the square. Partly for the sake of this symbolism coins are commonly used as Taoist implements. Heaven was also symbolized by the pi disc, made of jade and often marked with raised dots or spirals, which frequently symbolize the stars; it was in Chou and Han times laid on the back of the prone corpse at burial. Under the belly was laid the ts'ung, a tube of square section outside, cylindrical within. The energies of Heaven were also symbolized by constellations. These may appear as clusters of raised knobs, or, especially on robes and textiles, as dots linked by lines scattered over the field in which dragons fly. There are many star gods known to popular Taoism; their powers were harnessed in the design of charms. The forces of Earth are symbolized by certain animals, notably the tortoise, with its long streamers of trailing weed which the Chinese believed indicated vast age. Earth was also symbolized by the bronze cauldron-shape, and especially by the ancient ritual bronze vessels, already excavated from subterranean pre-Han tombs by the eighth century AD. The symbolism was interwoven with others.

This, broadly, is the pattern which yin-yang combination follows. But the polarity runs through the whole of Taoist art, worked out intensively and in great detail; more

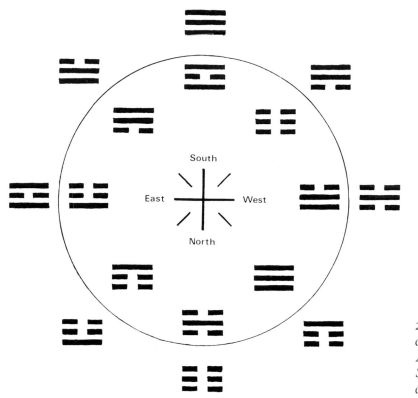

South

East
West

North

2 *Outer circle: the Sequence of Earlier Heaven, or Primal Arrangement. Inner circle: the Sequence of Later Heaven, or Inner World Arrangement*

instances will be discussed later, especially those connected with sexual and domestic imagery. It is developed into art by means of those two chief groups of imaginative unit mentioned earlier, by which the shapes of process in time are represented – cyclic patterns and threads or veins of energy.

The ancient oracle book the *I-ching*, the 'Book of Changes', fixed the cyclic patterns for Taoist art. It was one of the classics that all educated Chinese knew virtually by heart, and its interpretations and commentaries have long been treated by all philosophical schools as one of the profoundest philosophical texts in the Chinese tradition. At the same time it was used every day by professional fortune-tellers in the market-places of towns. It is based upon a set of eight trigrams, triplets of horizontal lines, either continuous or broken, which illustrate types or phases of change. Arranged in a circle (symbol of Heaven) they correspond with the compass directions, the times of day and the seasons of the year. Two chief circle systems are used, their significances complementing each other. The inner one is especially related to Taoist yoga. Continuous lines are yang, broken lines yin. Each trigram has a name, and a general symbolic significance which derives from interpretations and projections of the proportion of yang and yin it contains, and its 'seasonal' place in the two circles. None represents a permanent state; each is the herald of its successor. Many sets of paintings were made in China designed to express the subtle, shifting qualities of the trigrams through landscape or flower images; and the essential features of the trigrams were also represented by symbolic animals *(plate 25)*.

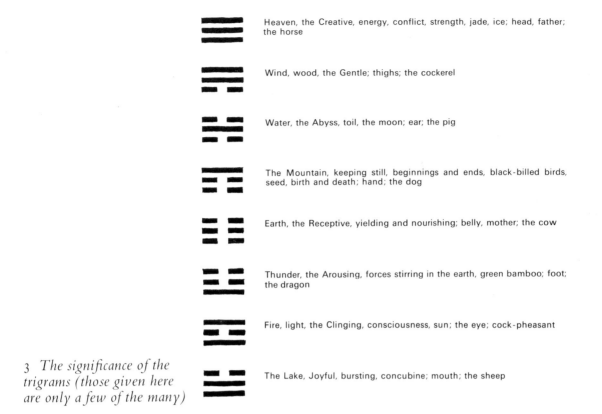

Heaven, the Creative, energy, conflict, strength, jade, ice; head, father; the horse

Wind, wood, the Gentle; thighs; the cockerel

Water, the Abyss, toil, the moon; ear; the pig

The Mountain, keeping still, beginnings and ends, black-billed birds, seed, birth and death; hand; the dog

Earth, the Receptive, yielding and nourishing; belly, mother; the cow

Thunder, the Arousing, forces stirring in the earth, green bamboo; foot; the dragon

Fire, light, the Clinging, consciousness, sun; the eye; cock-pheasant

The Lake, Joyful, bursting, concubine; mouth; the sheep

3 The significance of the trigrams (those given here are only a few of the many)

The *I-ching* oracles are consulted either by counting out yarrow stalks, or by casting three coins, so as to build up, line by line from below, two trigrams, one above the other. The resulting six-lined hexagram giving the 'answer' is felt to be an image of motion, which can be traced from the qualities of and the relations between the lines, and especially from the ascending series of four trigrams that each hexagram contains within it. Certain results cause one hexagram to generate a second, indicating a further phase of change to come. These hexagrams have been the subject of intense study by generations of scholars, and the text that goes with every one is a distillation of Chinese thought on the subject of change in time. Each represents a profound interweaving of changing relationships between yang and yin. Perhaps the most important question of all is: how can the oracles be conceived to work? For there is no doubt that they do, and they have always been taken absolutely seriously by the Chinese. This question will be answered later, after other things have been explained.

The hexagrams, their component trigrams, and the accompanying text, are probably the only attempts ever made in any culture to define the possible shapes of process in terms of unbroken duration. They do not express change as a mere shift from one 'state' to another. Their images have been evolved by correlating all the dominant constant cycles in which men are immersed – day and night, winter and summer, the apparent motions of the stars. Because these images have to give relevant answers to every actual question, the texts interpreting them are bound to seem very general. They become lucid the moment they are related to an actual case. The text will tell the individual how, for him, the vortices in the Tao are running. He can then, like the old man in the raging river, adapt himself to the present and coming shapes of change in which he swims. Harmony is again the ideal.

Both the physical appearance and the sense of the trigrams and the hexagrams are very common material for art. Together they are an image for the whole Tao. Individually, perhaps combined in significant ways, they appear on works of art made for particular rituals, celebrations or occasions (documentary plates 30–36). Their very presence induces the harmony with a particular phase of the Tao.

The directional symbolism in the circle of trigrams was extremely important in Chinese life, governing in particular the design of houses. For the Chinese always wished to 'face' the south, where lay the peak of yang vitality, with east and dawn on their left, west and dusk on their right, and north and midnight, the abyssal depth of yin, at their backs. Hence all who could afford to, built their courtyard-houses opening to the south. Temples were constructed similarly, their main altars raised up, facing to the south. Animals symbolizing the directions were used again and again in art, either as a group or individually, in paintings for example. They are: east, when yang is rising, the green dragon; south, when yang is at its peak, the 'phoenix' or 'red bird', a brilliant mythical long-tailed bird, which the Chinese pheasant with its gorgeous plumage symbolized in reality; west, when yin is taking over, the white tiger, which was also sometimes associated with winter and the north; and north, when the dark abyss of yin is dominant, the so-called 'dark warrior', a tortoise entwined and coupling with a snake (plate 24). Chinese bronze mirrors (plate 15) – extremely important personal possessions – often bear this set of symbols on their backs, sometimes associated with a square, at the centre of which the Earth-tortoise forms the knob; and, since they are usually circular, the symbolic meaning is at once obvious: the round, bright, reflecting side symbolizes the clear circuit of Heaven. Occasionally mirrors are themselves square, and bear the same group of emblems, which combines the image of square Earth with that of bright Heaven.

One aspect of Chinese art which was always taken very seriously in China has never been recognized in the West. This is the symbolism of materials. It is related to the strange, and apparently unschematic set of Taoist 'elements' described below, as well as to the doctrines of alchemy – a system of thought deeply rooted in Taoism. Mircea Eliade has beautifully demonstrated in his book *The Forge and the Crucible* what the processes of physical transformation which smelters, bronze-casters and smiths perform were felt to be, at bottom, in other places as well as China. The actions men carry out on natural materials were a speeding-up of 'ripening' processes going on in the earth anyway. Veins and lodes of metal were felt to be continuously condensing, very slowly, from the surrounding earth as a kind of 'essence of earth'. In a similar way, artists were supposed to manipulate and bring to a special kind of fruition the essences of the elements condensed into other materials.

The elements are: earth, wood, fire, metal, water. They, too, may be correlated with the directions and their trigrams, respectively: centre, east, south, west, north. But this correlation is only one of several possible; another important one is with the internal organs in Taoist yoga. It will be obvious that among the meanings of the trigrams of the Changes all the 'elements' are already included, along with other putative elemental states such as 'wind', 'mountain', 'thunder' and 'heaven'. What is important for Taoist art is that the states of change embodied in the elements and trigrams have, so to speak, essential substances or material forms. The materials of which works of art are made thus contribute to their symbolism. Metal and wood are obvious 'transformation stages' of the yin-yang dialectic; special woods, such as bamboo, pine or fruitwoods have their own particular meanings. Lacquer, which is the juice of a tree *(Rhus vernicifera)*, is an essence of wood. Stone and clay are essence of earth. Clay is used for making 'yin-receptive' pots, by means of fire; some stones may embody concentrated essence from other trigrams. Jade, however, is special, not an earth-stone; for it is the congealed semen of the dragon deposited on earth. Hence it is the essence of Heaven. As such it is used for innumerable images which embody the celestial power, many of which will be found among the illustrations. The essence of fire is symbolized on all kinds of art by the flame-shapes, even by black ink and black lacquer, which all Chinese know are made from the carbon soot deposited by burning pinewood on a smooth, cool surface. Water plays so fundamental a part in all artistic processes, from the painter's ink to the potter's clay, that its contribution to artistic symbolism is obvious. This is in addition to the deep and all-pervading significance already described.

So much for the grouped images of change. The second class of imaginative units for representing time is less clear-cut, more impalpable, but no less essential. These are the threads, veins or currents which are felt to pervade heaven, earth, all things, animals and people, giving rise to their individual characteristics and histories. Here again the image of water and its vortices is apt for the Tao. Water flows continually, and, in a sense, it can be said to be made up of myriads of currents or lines of flow, which all contribute to the process and rhythmic patterns in the whole. But air, with its currents, has likewise been used as an image for the pervading Tao. Smoke and clouds reveal the shapes of the currents in air. Their wandering coils, billows and strands resemble those less easily visible among the vortices in currents of water. The energies in time which constitute the Tao are thus thought to be analogous to – but not identical with – the currents in water and air. The skilful Taoist harnesses himself to them and rides them. The great artist makes them visible in all sorts of ways. The essential point is that they are 'independent of form', although there can be no appearance of form without them. They are real in a sense which binds the subjectivity of the spectator to the objectivity of his world. There is, in Taoist art, no such thing as abstraction; for to create linear shapes which do not directly illustrate an objective world would be pointless.

Direct presentations of these threads or veins in Chinese art follow the deeply coiling and convoluted paths of flowing water, or smoke eddying in the air *(plates 2, 5)*. But since in the Tao such currents are the vehicles of shapes and forms, they are also used as the basis of all true representation, even though they may not be represented obviously themselves. In Taoist works of art one has to look for them as much in implicit, as in actual visible lines. Many three-dimensional objects are marked with streaks or patches which illustrate these invisible currents penetrating the object *(documentary plate 51)*. Grouped blotches of coloured glazes on ceramics, stream-like or combed marbling of the ware, or patches and threads of gold on bronze ritual vessels, symbolize the paths taken by veins of subtle energy passing as time through three-dimensional space. And this notion gives meaning to that Chinese cult of stones with streaks, fur or feather-like markings, or wandering veins of chemical colour. They represent visible traces of the ancient Tao at work, not confined within individual things, but permeating them all.

Such mobile threads are especially significant in both three-dimensional and two-dimensional landscape art. They are the secret of the appeal of the great surviving Japanese gardens, such as the famous rock and sand complex at the Ryoan-ji temple in Kyoto or the Daisen-in of the Daitoku-ji *(plate 16)*. The veins running through landscape are studied by the aesthetic science known to the Chinese as the geomantic system of Feng-shui, that is, 'wind and water'. This science of geomancy studies the currents of the subtle energy of the Tao which permeate all landscapes with their hills, rocks, trees and rivers. In the management of actual terrain the Taoist idea was that the currents present in the earth since ancient times should always be preserved. When a well was to be sunk or a grave, house or road made, skilled diviners were called in to work out the correct locations and paths, to avoid 'disturbing the sleeping dragons', as the common expression puts it. The results would always respect the essential irregularities of the landscape and its organic features like cliffs, big trees or bluffs. This is, of course, totally opposed to Western ideas.

Landscape art in China summarizes symbolically the whole, moving Tao. The landscape artist had to induce a deep sense of 'dragon veins' running in all directions – including that of time – through the objective world presented in his work. The garden artist needed to study the individual rocks he was going to use, to intuit the veins implicit in their structure. He would then combine his groups by blending and harmonizing these veins, picking up the invisible curves and coils projected from one rock across intervening open space into those of other rocks. Paths and carefully shaped hillocks could follow and generate their own less emphatic veins according to the artist's knowledge of Feng-shui. The Westerner, though he may know little of the theories, nevertheless feels the presence of such subtle relationships in fine Far Eastern gardens.

The painter of two-dimensional landscapes aimed at something similar. He did not start with *actual* rocks as the gardener did; for Chinese and Japanese landscape paintings are always invented from the bottom up. Any study of nature that artists made was aimed at deciphering how the forces worked through things, not at copying outward appearances. The painter tried to suggest between his craggy mountains, hills and rocks, even as he invented them, skeins of linear connection. The forces which shaped the trees had to be demonstrated in their forms. Three-dimensional dragon-veins would wind back into the depths of the picture, as though they were threads on which the volumes were strung like beads *(plate 44)*. The represented objects should also be woven into a two dimensional unity, linked across the open painting surface by invisible, rhythmic connecting-lines. Han and Six Dynasties pictorial art even wove its images of mountains, animals and men out of continuous, undulating lines *(plate 5)*. Chinese criticism has always judged the quality of art by its success in creating this time-line unity.

Calligraphy is probably the most important artistic carrier of this sense of movement in time and change. The script in which Chinese is written consists of thousands of characters, each one being made up of a definite group of strokes. The strokes in each character are drawn always in the same order; the characters run down the page in columns from top to bottom, arranged in succession from right to left. One character (occasionally two) corresponds to a word. In formal scripts the characters are written carefully, so that each time a character appears it looks virtually the same. But there is also a group of styles (called 'cursive', and 'grass') used especially for verse or artistic prose, which make a special feature of incorporating 'a meaning beyond the text' *(plates 18, 52)*. That is to say, they allow the hand, prompted by the momentary intuition or inner spirit of the writer, to execute a vivid dance across the paper. In this dance the traces left by the gestures convey their own extra meaning. Individual characters look different, though written with the same general stroke-pattern, each time they appear; for their context is different. The characters are connected by a linear continuity which may be invisible where the brush-tip has left the paper, or visible where it has stayed in contact. Each linked group of strokes becomes an expressive kinetic trace which has never been written like that before, and never will be again. The 'meaning beyond the text' is a resonance evoked by traces, each of which is unique.

The brushwork may suggest, for example, 'the plunging of great whales', 'a stone falling from a precipice' *(plate 19)*, 'a vine trailing from a thousand-foot peak'. Such metaphors indicate how resonance can point beyond the text. The inner spirit of the inspired calligrapher projects it through his brush-movements that embody essential threads in the Tao, to which he is attuned. Someone who studies a piece of fine calligraphy can, by a sort of empathy, read back from the script to re-experience for himself the writer's original intuition. In the Far East this kind of expression and appreciation has immense depth, range and sophistication. Minute differences of personality and mental state can be conveyed by a creative writer, and grasped by a perceptive reader. The text itself may be an original composition, or simply the rewriting of a piece of conventional wisdom. Obviously to read a poem in a poet-calligrapher's own hand can be especially rewarding; but a great calligrapher can put his own realization of deep meaning even into a piece of fairly hackneyed text. Western graphology is a pale reflection of this Chinese art.

Official Taoism, in fact, evolved most beautiful secret scripts of its own *(plates 22–3)*. The *Tao-tsang* is full of them. The characters are quite different from those used in ordinary Chinese script, but follow a similar pictographic method. Their shapes coil or angle, and can be combined into powerful designs. The secrecy may have been partly due to the need to keep the details of Taoist cult from hostile eyes. But the real reason for the existence of such scripts was the fact that the meanings to which they referred simply had no true parallels in the concepts of ordinary language. The processes of cosmic time, the workings of the forces of Earth and Heaven, the inner realities of sexual mysticism and meditative practice, could only be designated by special graphic signs. They have an obvious aesthetic power; and the inner qualities of the secret conceptions that some of them express visually can be picked up by people interested in art, once they know what they are looking for.

Their chief use was in the writing of secret location diagrams and charms for special occasions. But they provided a vast repertoire of forms for artistic development. And it is already clear (though much more work on the subject is needed) that shapes appearing in many post-Sung works of art actually have special meanings derived from the patterns of these scripts. Incidentally, and very important, the script includes musical and smell notations.

True calligraphic expression is carried over into Chinese painting. If the spectator does not 'read' the brush strokes in a picture as they were written, following their movement with his eye – even with sympathetic movements of his hand – his own inner Vital

Spirit will not be stimulated to pick up all that the artist wished to express. For the great artist can both attune himself to the threads and vortices and then transmit them. China's greatest landscape painter of the early Sung, Li Ch'eng, who lived about 916–967, was looked on by his contemporaries virtually as a natural force; for by the richness of his imagination and brushwork he showed himself to be totally pervaded by the complex energies of the Tao *(plates 40, 41)*.

Landscape painting executed in black ink – perhaps with washes only of pale colour – was the art, after calligraphy, in which the Chinese were able to express most adequately their sense of Tao. There were, of course, major masters like Mu Ch'i and Liang K'ai who were Zen Buddhist monks; others like Ni Tsan were avowed Neo-Confucianists. But they shared a common method which distinguishes them from all other artists, Eastern or Western. The most important artistic point in this whole book follows.

The strokes and accumulated touches set down by all great Chinese painters in the open space of their pictures never claim to enclose, limit or define any things composing the real world. They may express the qualities of movement that give 'life' to a bird or plant, to a rock or landscape. But every mark laid on the surface of silk or paper is there in the first place to convert the empty surface into a visible crystallization of limitless Tao. Although, of course, 'placing' matters, in principle Taoist pictures use the objects they depict to convey a sense of the infinite space and undefined possibility which stretch out beyond their borders, both before and behind the surface. They indicate the infinity of the environment, and never confine their thoughts within the picture format. Large stretches of blank silk or paper may seem to become mist, cloud, sky or standing water *(plate 40)*. But really the brushed picture converts them into an actual image of the subtle fabric upon which reality itself is embroidered.

This effect can become particularly impressive when the painted surface is not simply flat, but three-dimensional – as with ceramics – or mobile – as with textiles. Symbolic objects depicted on an open space which follows the sophisticated curves of a piece of porcelain can develop very complex images. A painted dragon, for example, coiling around a vase occupies a region of three-dimensional space (as a dragon would) which is also defined by the surface of the pot-body; if it is painted *in reserve* (i.e., by being left blank and havings its background painted in a symbolic colour around it) such an image can become even more subtle. The surface painted on becomes one condensation or crystallization of the infinitely complex geometry of the continuum of space and time we inhabit but cannot normally see. For it stretches, undefined and limitless, far beyond all our possible frames of reference.

At least since the Sung dynasty it seems that one of the functions of the court painters of the Empire was to paint the robes used in court ceremonial with appropriate images, many based on landscape. Some famous old paintings which we now know as silk panels may have begun life in this form. The ceremonies were cosmic – for the emperor's function was to 'regulate' the cosmic process. They consisted of rituals which were complex versions of ordinary everyday domestic sacrifices. Few people realize how frequent and complicated Chinese rituals were, or how vitally important they were felt to be in keeping the whole of society in harmony with the Tao.

For the regular seasonal ceremonies the imagery was, of course, seasonal, closely related to the circuits of the *I-ching* trigrams. Diviners, magicians and observers, who must, virtually by definition, have been Taoists, were always an essential part of a court-establishment. It was their function to keep the court in contact with the processes of the changes as they appeared in natural and political events, and advise on the orientation and revision of ritual. A weather-manual used by such a Taoist observer throughout a year is illustrated here *(plate 9)*. The ceremonies carried out according to their joint recommendations would often call for variations in the qualities, colours, designs and even the materials of the costumes and vessels used, in the formulae of the liturgy, and the charms employed. Imperial edicts often enforced essential changes in public ritual. The ways in which the various objects used in such rites could influence each other, and combine to influence events in the world, were carefully studied. For the control at Imperial level of such influences was supposed to produce harmony throughout the Empire, eliminating the possibility or subduing the effects of 'natural disasters'.

In a similar way, good pictures could work their own positive magic on the world and people who looked at them. This, it should now be obvious, was not a matter of mere aesthetic enjoyment, but of lifting the spirit into a higher state. Most great Chinese landscapes are quite definite in their seasonal significance *(documentary plates 38–41)*; indeed many of them illustrate phases from the Changes. Album-sets often depict the qualities of all eight trigrams. The objects represented in a painting will have their proportions of yang and yin carefully combined and harmonized. Mountains, light and dark, water falling from above, in waterfalls, or sculpturing the valleys, drawn with lines and touches full of special quality, dry or wet, match the seasonal proportions of the Change. In temples and private houses the right pictures, like the right clothes and ceremonies, needed to be in evidence to keep the social units in harmony with the skeins of the Tao.

Chinese sculpture similarly works to reveal the Tao in our everyday space-time continuum. This gives it its own unique character – which again Westerners may find unsympathetic at first. The fundamental idea is seen most easily in the shapes of some of the superb wooden stands carved during the last few centuries for jades and porcelain. They emulate the twisting coils of tangled roots (sometimes they are carved from actual roots), or the interlacing of tree branches *(plate 47)*. For, of course, each such unique shape of natural growth explores the three-dimensions of space-as-limitless-environment, and illustrates threads of continuity in time. Since about 1600 a major art of bamboo carving in a similar vein has existed. Straightforward sculpture of Taoist heroes, such as Lao-tzu *(plate 31)* or some of the Immortals, always avoids defining bodies and clothes in terms of the geometric volumes to which the Western eye is accustomed. It works with linear surfaces, developing them as functions of continually changing lines, so as to explore impartially the three dimensions of space. Since they deliberately avoid fixing conceptual 'stopping places', their total mobility can seem at first 'slippery', indefinite and elusive; but this was, to the Chinese, their essential quality.

Taoist visual art actually involves the other senses as well. This is because the Taoist knew that all his senses were vital media through which he must absorb those currents, waves and vortices. In rituals, of course, and in a complete aesthetic environment, all the senses were catered for. Music and food, gesture, a wide variety of incenses and perfumes were combined. But individual works of visual art are given, quite deliberately, qualities belonging to other sense-fields. In a painted waterfall, for example, cunningly contrived lines, which look at first like the drawing of water, actually reveal themselves as musical notation in the secret Taoist script *(documentary plate 79)*. Porcelain bowls were listened to, as well as felt and looked at. Streaked qualities of glaze were identified with drifting incenses; bronzes were smelled by conoisseurs; and, of course, every three-dimensional object was made to appeal as much to the sense of touch as to the eye. All such suggestions, and the images with which, say, food-vessels or incense burners might be decorated, were meant actually to 'feed' the beneficent energies they symbolize into a person's own energy-system. The Tao with its limitless ramification and transformations lies beyond the scope of any one of the senses; but it enters and nourishes the inner man through all his senses jointly, and the more the sense-channels through which the influences of art can flow the better.

In Taoism sex, medicine and mysticism are intimately woven together. The human body, like the world it inhabits, is permeated by energies. They pass through it from outside, sweeping its doings, thoughts and history along in their process. This is why and how the oracles are believed to work. For the very act of consulting the *I-ching* is itself a harmonizing act, bringing the mental world of the consuler into direct relationship with the pattern of currents in which he is immersed. This, incidentally, is also part of the meaning of Chinese communist drill-displays, with their flying ribbons and undulating masses of coloured banners *(plate 21)*. But each individual is also permeated and kept in existence by patterns of energy constantly circulating within his psychosomatic system. These are the material upon which traditional Chinese medicine works; the t'ai-chi exercises still performed by millions of Chinese *(documentary plate 102)* are also designed to stimulate these inner currents, whose locations are accurately mapped. The current-tracks over the surface of the body used in acupuncture (and moxa-burning) treatments are part of the same complex. For art, the most important factor is the central circulation-pattern on which Taoist meditation and yoga are based, and to which the sexual energies are harnessed.

From the outside the Taoist adept or meditator seems, to the ordinary person, to be a mixture of doctor and magician, a healer on to whom the ordinary man projects his deepest hopes. Chinese literature is full of descriptions of legendary Immortals, both men and women; and the most famous of these 'hsien' were portrayed over and over again in art with a kind of yearning admiration. Shrines were dedicated to some of them during their lifetimes. The popular mind imagined their goals as being a transcendent version of ordinary worldly success. They are able to live in a green-and-gold Paradise in the West, filled with blossoming trees and beautiful pavilions. They are carried up to join the Heavenly Imperial Court *(plates 33–4)* by celestial beings wearing feathered cloaks, in mysterious chariots. They may ride through the air, sometimes on cranes or dragons. This aspect of the legend is full of overtones of ancient shamanism. For hsien who have reached heaven may return to earth; but there are also hsien who, at least for a period, were earth-bound; and these are the ones about whom most of the stories are told. They may live on the fringes of society or in caves, perhaps among the deep woods and dense thickets of remote mountains.

There are a number of common features in such stories. The hsien are said to achieve their immortality primarily by a diet of drugs and essences; these they sometimes record in recipe books they hand on to favourite pupils. The chief drugs are 'cinnabar' and 'gold-juice'; the essences come from organic substances such as pine-needles, melon seeds, certain roots, fungus and angelica. The latter, of course, contained the energies of yang and yin in various proportions. The drugs were, in fact, symbolic of mysterious inner forces which the uninitiated materialistically identified with external substances; and it was an inner meditative process that was described as alchemical cooking or roasting of chemicals.

Another common factor in the tales about hsien is the way they are seen alive years, or even many centuries, after they were supposed to be dead. Relatives who exhume their bodies, to check, sometimes find that what had actually been buried was only a bamboo stick or a jade seal. Some hsien reincarnate repeatedly. Lao-tzu *(plate 31)*, the reputed author of the *Tao-te-ching*, is said to be reborn at least once every generation somewhere in China. Hsien perform miracles, eating boiled stones, bringing long-dead skeletons to life, travelling at lightning speed or producing armies of spirit soldiers from a blank wall. They rise to heaven or travel through the sky in broad daylight; for to them time and space are merely relative. They converse with star gods and perform successful major surgery. Everyone believes it possible to meet a hsien; and they are mentioned affectionately by some of China's greatest poets.

One of the best known hsien is Li T'ieh-kuai. He looks like a lame and repulsive beggar, carrying an iron staff and a gourd. This is because once, when his spirit left his body to visit Lao-tzu, his own fine body accidentally got burned; so he had to make use of that of a beggar who had died of starvation nearby. From his gourd a mysterious coiling vapour rises, in which appears an emblem of his true spirit. Another, Ma Shih-huang, was a horse doctor who performed acupuncture on a sick dragon, and cured him. So the dragon carried him off to immortality as a reward. Yet another, who always has with him his three-legged toad, is Liu-hai *(plate 28)*. He caught this wonderful beast when drawing water from a well. This toad is thus a symbol of deepest yin, which endows him with immense power. He sometimes carries a string of coins, so he is also the patron of commercial success.

Many of the features in these legends, in one way or another, are allegories for aspects of an underlying and hidden reality – the reality of Taoist meditation and Inner Alchemy which is described below. An interesting point is that all these saints and sages preserve their distinct outward individuality – even a grotesque eccentricity. Individuality is essential to the Tao; and there are sound metaphysical reasons why someone who achieves the Taoist goal should remain visibly unique.

Taoism, like other Oriental cults, assumes an equation between the outer world which a man inhabits and his inner self. Man and world are functions of each other, though most people do not normally realize it. Since the Tao permeates each man, it is possible for each to find the Tao reflected entire within himself and make it present to his inward intuition – if he knows how. The 'know-how' has two stages. First is the proper use of sex. Second is an inner meditative structure, a 'subtle body' made up of energies, providing each person with the means to achieve harmony with the Great Whole. This is then experienced as total tranquillity, and what is called 'immortality', for which the stork or crane *(plate 61)* is the symbol.

The Chinese have always taken it very much for granted that sex has a central place in life. Although Confucians may have disapproved of it being much discussed in public, in private relations between the sexes were a vital concern. Polygamy was normal, and well-to-do men would have concubines as well as wives. The emperor always had vast numbers of both wives and concubines of different grades. This was not merely for the sake of indulgence. At root it is probably a manifestation of the primitive idea of aristocracy. The underlying notion seems to be that the rights to land are symbolized by women, who were somehow identified with it, and thus had a natural title to it. Any man wishing to accumulate land naturally accumulated the title-holders as wives. But once polygamy had become institutionalized as a status symbol its origins were forgotten, though the deep underlying correlation between women, earth and yin remained. Within any polygamous household special conditions prevailed.

One man was obliged to satisfy sexually many women, without reducing himself to a state of exhaustion. It was not only his domestic peace that was at stake. A man whose household was in turmoil could lose a lot of public status, perhaps even his official position. All men therefore had to learn a large number of clever erotic techniques. The fundamental skill was for the man to be able to bring several women to frequent orgasms, without himself experiencing orgasm.

These are the ordinary facts. But they only show the outward aspect of Taoist belief, which is shaped by the theory of yin and yang. Taoist art, much of which was made for the domestic environment, is full of references to sex and sexual customs. The Taoist idea is that sexual essences are secreted by men and women, when they become sexually aroused. These essences are material forms of energies which in men are predominantly yang and in women yin. By orgasm the energies are released out of the body, and may be absorbed by the partner of the opposite sex, especially through their sexual organs.

Any follower of Tao, male or female, naturally aims at some sort of self-cultivation, even if it is only at a modest level. And Taoist self-cultivation, from the humblest effort right up to the peaks of spiritual achievement, is based upon manipulating sexual energy. Each individual needs his or her own inherent sexual energy – yang or yin – arousing to its maximum. But each man or woman also needs to receive generous doses of the energy of the opposite sex to travel far along the road of self-cultivation. This gives a strange ambiguity to Chinese sexual life. Erotic skills become exceptionally important, and many handbooks were written and illustrated. They gave careful instructions as to how often, at what times of day and seasons of the year, people of different ages should enjoy sex. But most important are their instructions as to how the act should be performed, so as to give the greatest benefit to all the participants – of whom there may be several.

Preliminary amorous play stimulates the yang and yin, and the secretions begin to flow. There are at least six styles of penetration. Then during intercourse men and women bring each other to the highest pitch of excitement and tension, using nine styles of movement and postures whose names in themselves are vivid poetical metaphors: 'seagull's wings over the cliff-edge', 'bamboos near the altar', 'goat butting the tree', 'reversed flying-ducks', 'wailing-monkey hanging from a pine tree', 'cat and mouse in one hole' *(see plates 38, 49–50)*. Alternating deep and shallow thrusts may follow the rhythm of 3-5-7-9. A slow thrust should be like 'the movement of a big carp caught on a hook', a quick one 'like a flight of birds against the wind'. Movements should be varied, and full of invention, suiting the moods and needs of both partners from moment to moment. They may be called by special names, such as, for example, 'prying open an oyster to reach the pearl', 'sparrow pecking rice-grains', or 'brave soldier flailing right and left to break the enemy ranks'.

The male and female sexual organs have names whose imagery forms part of the secret language of Taoism. The male is 'the red bird', 'the jade stalk', 'the coral stem', 'turtle-head', 'the heavenly dragon pillar' *(documentary plate 105)*, 'the swelling mushroom'. The female is 'the peach', 'the open peony blossom' *(plate 45)*, 'the vermilion gate', 'the pink shell', 'the golden lotus', or the 'receptive vase'. In fact the female yin symbolism of all ceramic vases is fully recognized in Taoist art. Sexual intercourse itself is referred to as 'the bursting of the clouds and the rain'. 'Plum blossom' *(plate 27)* – that subject painted tens of thousands of times on beds, screens and porcelain – is actually a *name* for sexual pleasure. The point is that all the objects referred to in these figures of speech are used in works of art both to indicate the sexual experiences for which they are metaphors, and to imbue the objects with the energies associated with the experiences. This accounts for the ways they may be grouped, and for the special kinds of graphic or colour emphases they may be given.

Sex carried out so intensively, and with such poetic care, enormously enhances the yang in men and the yin in women. As intercourse progresses men are able to drink from under the tongues and from the breasts of their partners special yin essences secreted there. But it is orgasm that releases the most potent essences. After orgasm has happened, these essences need to be carefully absorbed, drawn into himself from the female's depths through the man's penis, from the male's body into her vagina by the woman. After mutual orgasm skilled and generous lovers will make a complete exchange.

This may be delightful and beneficial as an act of love. However, in such mutual orgasm each partner loses his or her yang or yin essences to the other. There can be no doubt that, at many periods in Chinese history, such an exchange was regarded as a thoroughly valuable 'harmonization' of yang and yin, leading to long life and vigorous old age. But there was a more austere and demanding side to Taoist cult, which was followed by those who aimed at a total self-identification with the Tao. Its success depended on building up a powerful charge of both male and female essences in one person's own body. So a man or a woman who wished to climb the heights would first learn to limit his or her own orgasms, whilst coupling with and bringing to orgasm as many partners of the opposite sex as possible, so as to absorb their released essences. The partners had to be young, and so full of yang or yin; and in the end the Taoist adept might inhibit his or her own orgasms completely; though this extreme was thought to be dangerous by some Taoist schools. Obviously the ordinary well-to-do household gave splendid opportunities to its male head.

The goddess Hsi-wang-mu, who was said to live in the Peach-garden Paradise in the West, is the best known personification of female success *(plate 51)*. The star god Shou-lao, with a peach in his hands, is the prototype of male success *(plate 62)*; and everywhere in Chinese art the peach, with its deep cleft, alludes obliquely to the benefits for men produced from the vulvas of young girls. In a sense one could call all this a kind of sexual 'vampirism'. If the extreme theory is accepted there can be no point in a man and a woman who have equally high Taoist ambitions coupling with each other. But since such people of either sex were very rare, the problem scarcely arose; though folk tales do tell of strange 'contests'.

One special consequence follows from the deep sexual imagery in Taoist thought and art. Since human being and world were taken to be functions of each other, and since yin and yang essences distinguished the sexes, it was natural to assume a kind of sexuality pervading the outside world, which produced its own essences. Yang and yin combine in the cosmic trigrams and hexagrams of the *I-ching*. But here the polar energies are very abstract and intangible. The world the aspiring Taoist Immortal inhabited offered him many concrete things, which he could absorb to build up his inner complex of energies. Sights, sounds, smells and especially foods contain the yin and yang in different proportions, and so need to be taken at the right times in the right amounts. The environment itself can be, so to speak, sexually milked of its essences.

The Earth is the greatest repository of yin energies. The clouds and mist are – the Chinese held – exhaled towards Heaven as its breath *(plate 42)*. The yellow cup-shaped fungus (like a chanterelle) is a condensation of the Earth's yin. Therefore, in art, cloud and fungus share the same double-coiling shape, which signifies in general the wandering of yin currents. The energy returns from heaven as water, which comes down as rain, with its sign changed, and then seeks out the valleys and hollows to follow a wandering course, developing waves and whirlpools. Wooden stands for jade objects often represent whirling waves, as the yin counterpart to the yang stone, symbolizing the yin abyss. Other stands, embodying yin in the element of wood, may be carved to represent ranks of square (earth) rocks *(documentary plate 2)*, or tree or flower-stalks arranged in the pointed vulva-shape of the leaf of the artemisia bush.

The high mountain peak is where the Taoist 'mountain man' can absorb the bright yang airs of heaven, and meet the constellations face to face. Dew is also a heavenly essence, which Taoists should drink. Another mushroom, phallic in shape, also crystallizes yang. The horns of deer are yang-aphrodisiac; and so a deer in art may carry the complementary gift of yin fungus in its mouth *(plate 11)*. Rhinoceros horn, most powerful aphrodisiac of all, the excrescence of sheer yin, is used to make cups for mixing medicines. Their shapes suggest the female vulva, liquefying and dripping with yin-essence, and female dragons with divided 'vortex'-like tails adorn their handles.

Perhaps the most powerfully symbolic natural substance of all, which has a profound meaning, is cinnabar. This is a rosy-purple crystalline stone, sulphide of mercury. Ground up, it is the red pigment used in painting *(plate 9)*. But in Taoist symbolism and magic it represents the nuclear energy of joined yang and yin, which is to be fired in the internal crucible by alchemical yoga, to generate the yogi's immortality – just as mercury is produced from the rock by calcining it, when the sulphur releases a shining metallic fluid. A too materialistic interpretation of the 'benefits' of cinnabar led to the deaths of many Taoists, including even some Chinese emperors, who swallowed repeated doses and died of mercury poisoning.

Cinnabar is a key symbol in the most sophisticated mechanism of inner energies which the advanced Taoist builds up into a 'subtle body', and manipulates to reach his highest spiritual goal. This inner geography explains many of the cryptic allusions in Chinese poetry, mythology and art. It also proves decisively that alchemy, Chinese or Western, was not simply an infantile chemistry (as many scholars still imagine, who should know better) but was always an externalization of inner processes meant to synthesize man with his world. It was only popular misunderstanding and legend which made some Taoists believe that they could achieve immortality by grinding up drugs and herbs. The true compounded 'pill', the real elixir of life, was to be found inside, not out.

The Inner Alchemy of Taoism is closely related to the meditative practices of Indian Tantrik yoga; and there can be no doubt that Taoist meditative texts are full of terms and methods derived from the Buddhist forms of Tantra which flourished from time to time in China. But it is also obvious that, despite the borrowings, Taoist yoga springs fundamentally from its own native tradition, which is also full of reminiscences of shaman cult like that known until recently elsewhere in Asia. Such yoga is, in fact, the root and centre of the whole of Taoism, giving point to and clinching the meaning of the outward symbolism illustrated in this book. For genuine religions live in what their followers *do*, not in what they merely think and say. Incidentally, there are aspects of Taoist yoga which make sense of what have often been thought to be mere enigmatic phrases used by Zen Buddhists.

The Taoist subtle body which gives shape to the yoga is not as clear-cut and definite as the subtle body of Indian Tantra. It has been represented in art occasionally *(plate 53)*; but different Taoist sects have emphasized different functions, and some terms are deliberately ambiguous; so it is not possible to reduce all the variations to a single cut-and-dried scheme. This is typically Taoist. Simple schemata are regarded as vulgar and deceptive. But a general, inclusive pattern of meditative practice can be described, which is meant to take months or years to complete. And the processes of artistic creation are intimately linked with meditation. The former, indeed, reflect the latter.

One has always to remember that nothing in the Taoist universe, inner or outer, is static. Everything is dynamic process. Meditation always itself moves forward, and the Taoist who sits down to meditate enters a vast inner continuum of moving energies, in which the whole outer universe can be reflected. They have mysterious names, and interact not in simple, but in varied complex ways. When the inner universe is transformed by the Inner Alchemy, inner and outer are united, and the meditator experiences, as a matter of direct perception and knowledge, the Great Whole, the Tao, complete, unbroken, containing all change within its transcendent tranquility. Since he has gone beyond change he is rightly called an 'Immortal'. The character for 'shou', 'long life' (a modest immortality) became for all Chinese a kind of universal charm *(plates 52, 54)*, a fascinating reminder of the Taoist ideal, executed in every possible artistic medium, thousands of times over.

Transformation is the key to this yoga. Cinnabar is the emblem of what is transformed. The transformation takes place in three chief stages, in three 'crucibles', each of which is itself a transformation, and is located at a place on a central column within the body. The lowest is inside the belly, just below the navel. The second is behind the solar plexus; the third is in the head, behind and between the eyes. They are called tan-t'ien (Japanese *tanden*), meaning 'elixir-field'. The lowest is contained in a 'cauldron' or 'furnace' with three feet, which is kept stoked up with an inner fire at the lowest tan t'ien, almost to the end of meditation. This is the central function.

What is transformed in the crucibles, the 'substance' on which the alchemical firing and transforming process works, is the sexual energy, called ching. Late and bowdlerized texts describe how the meditator should abstain from sexual activity, and, like a miser, hoard his sexual energy. They teach that a man must regard his semen as his 'precious thing', and guard it carefully against 'loss'. Even today the Chinese people tend to believe that one's energy and stock of life are used up by sex. In meditation he should arouse himself, by manual stimulation of his own sexual organ if necessary, and draw up the aroused energy into the lowest crucible so that his organ shrinks. But there can be no doubt that full-fledged Taoist meditation goes far beyond this timid folklore, and calls not only for the individual's own aroused yang or yin sexual energy, but also for the massive doses of the energy of the opposite sex which can be absorbed through sexual intercourse. In fact, dedicated Taoists – as their enemies often pointed out in tones of pious horror – practised sexual intercourse as an integral part of their meditation. No man can reach the goal without receiving generous gifts of yin essence, no woman without yang. True Taoist ching was therefore an intimate accumulation of the energies of both sexes, nourished by elaborate sexual exchange. This was the 'alchemical substance', the essence around which the whole inner transformation revolved. In the lower tan-t'ien it could be split, for further processing, into four combinations of yang and yin *(plate 53)*.

The ching was one of a trinity of forces *(plate 13)*, each of which 'resided' in one of the three centres mentioned above, and also had a special part to play in artistic creation. The triple spiral which often appears on Taoist works of art refers to this trinity. The ching provided the aesthetic impulse, the motive power of artistic inspiration. The other two are: first, the ch'i, which is the moving vitality, located in the middle centre, the force by which great artists attune themselves to the movements of the Tao; and second the shen, or luminous personal spirit, compounded of all an individual's thoughts, feelings and sense of identity, which endows the artist with his personal style. This is located in the special cavity of the head called the upper crucible. Each of these three, ching, ch'i and shen, although personal at first, is capable of being transformed, by the alchemy of yoga, into the cosmic version of itself. In the expression of great art a similar transformation was achieved and presented.

The energy which is harnessed to fuel the transforming fire in the furnace is a transformation of the ordinary breath; or rather, the breath is the instrument the meditator uses to discover and arouse this inner energy. It takes the form of a subtle fire. The whole meditative process begins with regular, deep in-and-out breathing (the breath is not held, as in Indian yoga). The lowest tan-t'ien, the region of the vegetative energies, is correlated with Earth; the region of the 'heart', which in Chinese corresponds with the upper mental and emotional energies, is correlated with heavenly fire. As breathing progresses its own energy is transformed into an inner circulation. This, as it develops, picks up the energy of the heart-fire and carries it down into the 'furnace', where it is blown and amplified by further circulation. It begins to heat and transform the ching, which by now is gathered in the lowest crucible within the furnace.

The meditator starts the circulation by 'sending his thought' around a track which rises up from the base of the spine to the top of the head, and descends through the upper lip and the front of the chest, to the root of the sexual organ. From there it goes into the lowest crucible, helping the condensation of the ching. Then it sets off again to the base of the spine, and so on. The energy derived from the breath is gradually identified with the 'thought'. As the circulation becomes more vigorous, and the energy ceases to be mere 'thought', it becomes a true 'inner fire', and its channel becomes more definite. The spinal column, in particular, turns into a magnificent road of ascent to a range of magical mountains which rise beyond the head. These represent the ultimate home of the immortal 'mountain man'. The road up passes through three gates. The lowest is at the base of the spine; the second in the back; the third, the Jade gate, is where the spine joins the skull.

The whole circulation becomes a passage through twelve stages, each represented by one of the *I-ching* hexagrams. As the energy rises up the spine, so the yang content increases. As it descends down the front channel, so yin replaces yang. In art a dragon peering over the Taoist sage's head may represent this circulation *(plate 62)*. One important point is to distinguish very carefully between the stage through which the circulation passes at the top of the head, and the cavity of shen, the upper crucible. To confuse the two can spoil the whole operation.

The next phases bring the inner fiery circulation, fanned by numbered breathings, to high power. This generates an intense and purifying heat in the furnace. The ching, transformed in it, rises in its crucible, to become the middle tan-t'ien crucible, and combine with the ch'i, or Vital Energy. The two, united, continually drop back into the furnace for purification, then soar up the central column. Meantime the meditator has also aroused the inner light of the shen in its cavity between, behind and a little above the eyes. He stirs it, by rolling and stimulating the eyes, into a circulation of its own within a pattern of channels. By this circulation the 'mysterious gate' of individuality opens before the inner sight, and the meditator's own 'face before he was born' appears to him. This is why Chinese sages so often have 'dragon eyes'.

With these two circulations in full swing, the great 'Inner copulation of Dragon and Tiger' suddenly takes place *(plate 66)*. The shen in the head transforms into the golden

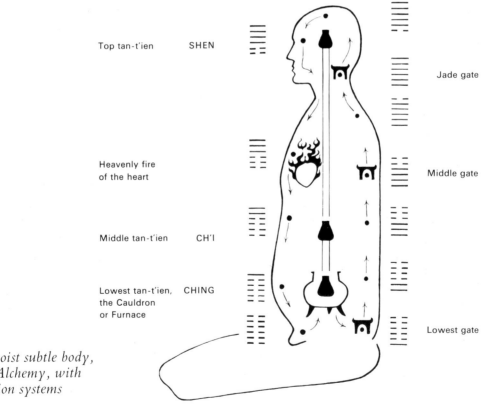

Top tan-t'ien SHEN

Jade gate

Heavenly fire of the heart

Middle gate

Middle tan-t'ien CH'I

Lowest tan-t'ien, the Cauldron or Furnace CHING

Lowest gate

4 The Taoist subtle body, for Inner Alchemy, with its circulation systems

elixir, and flows down the centre channel into the lowest crucible, there to combine with the fused ching and ch'i for a further, critical, firing.

Now follows the process whereby the joined trinity is transformed from personal to cosmic. Around the crucible in which all three are now being cooked, while the great circulation of inner fire keeps the furnace at purifying heat, a second fiery circulation starts around the region of the lowest tan-t'ien. This may, in fact, be one of the oldest ingredients in the yoga; for it makes use of the five ancient elements, earth, wood, fire, metal, water, with their directional significance and their association with a symbolic group of internal organs. Earth, centre, is in the spleen; wood, east, in the liver; fire, south, in the heart; metal, west in the lungs; water, north in the kidneys. It is probable, however, that this cosmicizing process could also involve the entire circuits of the trigrams, as they appear in the I-ching. Their elemental energies then unite into a ring or lotus of cosmic fire orbiting the furnace of the lower tan-t'ien.

The fused and transformed ching-ch'i-shen substance then rises up the mid-channel to the topmost crucible. Circulating there, it, so to speak, intersects with the vast orbit of the Original cosmic ch'i and shen of the Tao. From this meeting a pair of liquid radiances flower, one named silver and one named gold, sometimes moon and sun. A special ambrosia gathers in the mouth like saliva. This must be swallowed down the front subtle channel into the lowest crucible. It is the cosmic negative energy. In the lowest crucible it congeals into the Seed of Immortality. As the two lights slide down the central column to join it there, all outward breathing stops. The great circulation, which all this while has fanned the fire in the furnace, ceases, and silent, motionless 'foetal breathing' takes over. Slowly the lights infuse the seed, to generate a Taoist 'foetus', within the orbit of the cosmic energies. The breath this foetus breathes comes from the beyond. As it is carefully matured it grows into a 'crystal child', and rises, enveloped in the cosmic energies, into the head. There, one day, it combines with them; individual life and original nature fuse in one. From the crown of the skull emerges the new-born Immortal.

Such is the course of the Inner Alchemy. Its geography can be abbreviated and, of course, expanded and extended. The texts are full of technical advice, and additional or alternative patterns of dialectic. Folklore and popular belief have focused on and visualized the nuclear images, and these are the subject matter of the art illustrated in this book.

To begin with, the lowest tan-t'ien, just below the navel, is immensely important. Every Far Eastern sage or hero is shown with an ample, strong but relaxed belly. It is the root of all his energy. Still today the Japanese cultivate the virtue they call 'hara', 'belly', as evidence of a well-developed 'tanden'. The traditional Chinese culture-hero is not a young man with a flat belly, who wastes his essence in constant erotic orgasms, but an old man whose healthy looks show that he knows how to husband his resources, and, incidentally, to make a large number of women happy according to their lights. The Taoist deity Shou-lao is always represented with his skull vastly enlarged by its content of transformed energy (plate 62). Art illustrates Immortals riding on dragons or tigers. They may carry significant objects such as peaches or ju-i sceptres, which are shaped like the cloudy coils of yin-essence (plate 65). A very common subject is the Taoist 'infant' (plate 64), either alone or playing with others, perhaps in the Peach-garden Paradise in the West, presided over by the yin goddess Hsi-wang-mu. They may be playing with toys that are emblematic of the currents of cosmic energy, such as bamboo wind-instruments, or miniature weapons standing in a vase. Taoists may wear a special cap worked in the shape of yin cloud-fungus *(plate 63)*, ornamented, perhaps, with small yang antlers, jewels and a flying bobble. The natural home of the Taoist wise-man is among the mountains. There, in a landscape which is a projection of the Tao itself, he will learn to live off pine-kernels and fungus, to drink the dew and be impregnated by the rain of heaven. He will thus absorb yang and yin energies in their cosmic, not merely their human, form.

Far and away the most common and least understood of the symbols derived from Taoist cult is the flaming 'pearl' or gem with which dragons play on thousands of paintings, jades, ceramics *(plate 60)* and embroidered robes *(plate 55)*. The 'pearl' represents the essence of yin and yang condensed into ching and ch'i, sexual energy and vital force, at once human and cosmic, enveloped in the fire of transformation. The dragons symbolize the creative energies which are compressed within the 'pearl', and from it generate the cosmos. Ming and Ch'ing emperors, who took this as their emblem, intended so to demonstrate that they owned the creative power of the universe, which they claimed to mediate for their subjects. Experienced Taoists would understand it as the image of a process with which they were individually familiar. For in Taoism, as in all other religious conventions, what the meditator experiences and describes as an inner ascent is a reversal of the processes of what the outer world sees as cosmic 'creation'. The adept personally returns to the source of things.

The masses of the people inevitably saw the Taoist yogi as a magician. To them it seemed natural that someone who could identify himself with the energies of the universe should be able to control at least the more modest problems of human life. And there were plenty of serious Taoists, throughout history, who saw their task to be using their powers as best they could for the benefit of their fellow men. They included teachers and doctors, some of whom spent years wandering in the remote mountains collecting herbal remedies. The Chinese pharmacopaeia of herbal drugs has still not been thoroughly investigated; though acupuncture, another product of the Taoist understanding of reality, is becoming steadily better known in the West. There were also, undoubtedly, large numbers of quacks and frauds who played on popular superstition; and it was always easy for opponents of Taoism to find sticks to beat genuine Taoists with. But the fortune-tellers who sat in the market-places and temple courtyards manipulating the hexagrams of the *I-ching*, and the priests who wrote elaborate charms in the Taoist secret script, either against diseases and misfortune or to produce beneficial effects, spiritual and physical, were certainly working with the most serious intentions. They used their apparatus to decipher the movements of the Tao as they understood them, and harness the world's energies to alleviate men's fears, so helping them to harmonize their actions with the turbulent vortices of existence.

It is also, however, true that all this manipulation of energies is, in the final Taoist resort, absurd. For to labour self-consciously to attain longevity was itself a cause of spiritual failure. The struggle itself implied a fundamental error. The ultimate hope of every genuine Taoist was to reach that state of tranquillity beyond time and change which *is* the Tao, the Uncarved Block, the Great Whole. He knew he could only reach it by becoming, in a sense, one with time and change, and learning to stop behaving and feeling as if he were a separate independent agent. It was a natural testimony to human anxiety that the aim of Taoism should be designated 'long life' or 'immortality'. For anyone who has studied the *Chuang-tzu* book knows perfectly well that the human body vanishes, dissolved like everything else in the process of change. The 'crystal infant' and the Immortal riding the currents of Tao are figurative or analogical devices for laying hold of and controlling experiences and inner phenomena for which there are no other terms.

It is no easy matter to transform oneself completely and live in permanent awareness of the truth of Tao. Chinese poets have recorded again and again their longing pursuit of such tranquillity. Enlightened artists have found images to capture its presence *(plate 67)*. It is the intrinsic meaning of all that is greatest in China's art. But the innumerable Taoist calligraphers who devoted their art to writing beautifully 'wu-wei', 'non-action', knew very well the enormous difficulty of reaching the condition of spirit to which those two characters refer. It cannot be seized by any act of will. The whole apparatus of Taoist magic, mysticism and philosophy was devised for the express purpose of mapping approaches to that pinnacle of apparent simplicity. Its taste is like cool spring water; it experiences no obstructions, no divisions; it looks like the limpid air. It has no pretensions and makes no claims. From its vantage point, yesterday and tomorrow are equal, and so are ant and emperor. The most distant age is no further off within the Tao than the moment just slipped away.

A passage in the Book of Chuang-tzu describes true Taoist sages. They are those who pursue the natural way of heaven and earth, who cultivate themselves without indulging in 'benevolence' or 'righteousness', and succeed without fame. They attain longevity without cultivating the breath. Their qualities are identical with the ultimate substance of the Tao – placidity, indifference, silence, tranquillity, emptiness, and non-action. They are evenly balanced and at ease; anxieties and evil find no access to them, nothing unpleasant can take them by surprise. The life of each sage is like the turning of heaven; his death is the transformation common to all things. In stillness his virtue is yin, in diffusion it is yang. He takes no initiative to produce either happiness or disaster; he responds to each influence, and moves as he feels pressure, acting when he must. He discards conventional wisdom and all memories of the past, following harmoniously the lines of heaven. His life is a floating, his death a resting.

1 Carved jade mountain with the three star gods of Longevity, Prosperity and Happiness of popular Taoism being worshipped by pilgrims to the sacred mountain. The kidney-shape is symbolic of the female (yin) vulva and is harmonized with the male (yang) substance of jade and the mountain shape. Early eighteenth century, Ch'ing dynasty, h. $5\frac{5}{8}$ in.

2 Marbled design representing the flow of Vital Energy (ch'i), on a Celadon dish of the fourteenth century, Ming dynasty, d. $10\frac{1}{4}$ in.

3 'Jade mountain' seal of phallic shape with landscape design, sun disc (yang) and clouds (yin). Eighteenth century, Ch'ing dynasty, soapstone h. $4\frac{3}{8}$ in.

4 Model of a landscape garden with pool and undulating rocks. Three-colour glazed earthenware, T'ang dynasty, recently excavated in China

5 The inlaid gold on this bronze hill-jar represents continuous Vital Energy like rising smoke, developing into a three-dimensional landscape. Western Han dynasty (209–6 BC), h. 9½ in.

6 *Diagram of Change*, representing the penetrating force of the Vital Spirit, the action of the transcendental Tao, and the links between the macrocosm and the microcosm. Northern Sung dynasty. Reproduced from the Taoist Canon *(Tao-tsang)*

7 Dragon-fish: the change of the yin fish into the yang dragon, symbolizing the waxing yang and the waning yin spirit. Glazed pottery roof ornament from a Taoist temple. Early nineteenth century, Ch'ing dynasty, h. 9½ in.

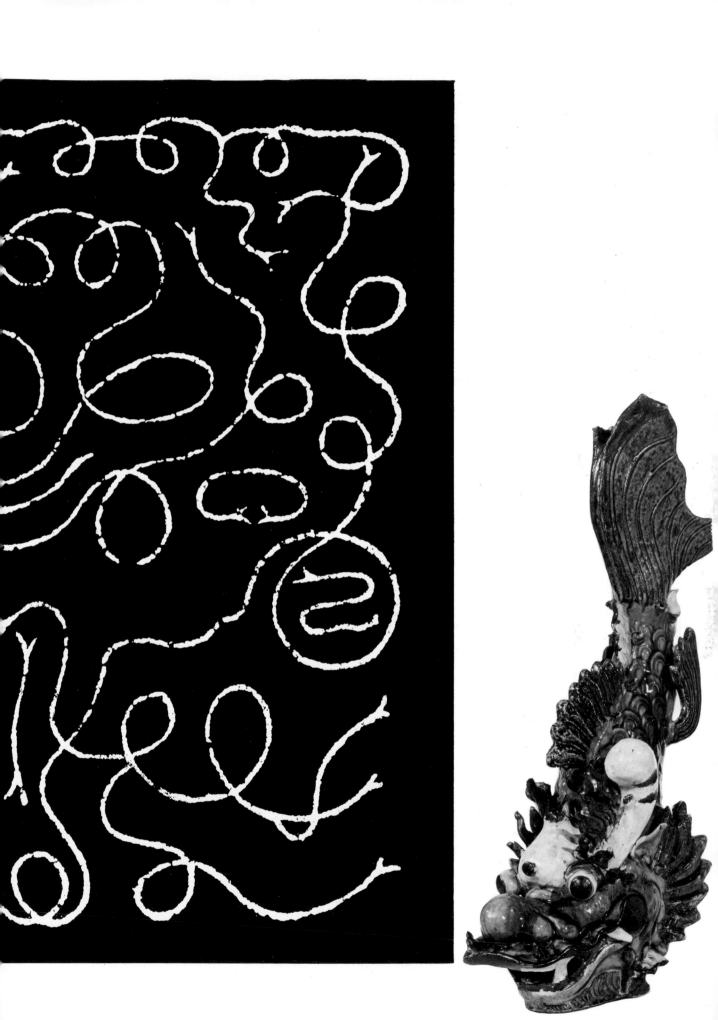

8 Magic spirit fungus (ling-chih) on an egg-shell porcelain vase. The vase is symbolic of the female sex organ, while to eat the spirit fungus was believed to give immortality for at least five hundred years. Shape and decoration together imply the life-prolonging effect of sexual intercourse. Four-character Yung-cheng mark (1723–35), but twentieth century, h. $7\frac{7}{8}$ in.

9 Fire (yang) and cloud (yin) combined, a phase of evolving Vital Energy, on a nineteenth-century Taoist weather-manual. Ink and cinnabar on paper $9\frac{1}{2} \times 6\frac{1}{4}$ in.

歘火會雷霆大鬫雷電大作折樹誅妖驟雨傾盆

10 The dragon emblem
of yang, a gilt bronze
ritual staff-head, *c.* 1800,
Ch'ing dynasty, h. 5¼ in.

11 The Immortal Lan
Ts'ai-ho walking among
yin clouds with her
flower-basket and
accompanied by a deer
holding ling-chih fungus
in its mouth. Regarded
as a goddess she per-
sonifies the extreme of
yin, personal and cosmic.
Carved soapstone seal of
kidney shape. Late
seventeenth century,
Ch'ing dynasty, h. 9⅜ in.

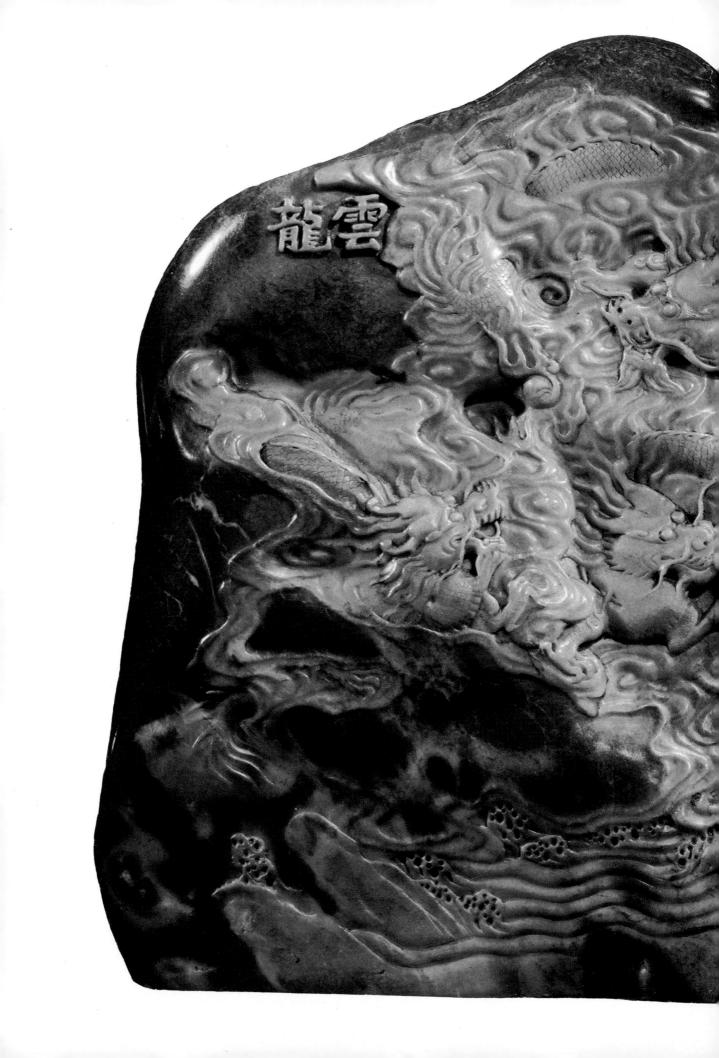

龍雲

12 Dragon (yang) in clouds (yin). Eighteenth century, Ch'ing dynasty. Soapstone h. 7 in.

13 The fluid glaze in the bottom of this sacrificial bowl (yin) suggests three penis (yang) forms, symbolizing the unity of Heaven, Earth and Man, as well as the inner alchemical triad. Kwantung stoneware imitation of Sung Chün ceramic. Sixteenth century, Ming dynasty, d. $7\frac{3}{4}$ in.

15 Cosmic mirror decorated with the four directional animals symbolizing the cycle of time. Silvered bronze, T'ang dynasty, d. $10\frac{1}{2}$ in.

14 Jade bell. In the vertical band is the Great Ultimate (i.e. interlocking yin-yang) symbol at the centre, with celestial pi disc and ch'ien trigram above. K'un below represents Earth, the receptive. Horizontal bands of cloud spirals and constellation bosses enclose a central band decorated with triple circles representing the unity of Heaven, Earth and Man. Twelfth to thirteenth century, Sung dynasty, h. $4\frac{5}{8}$ in.

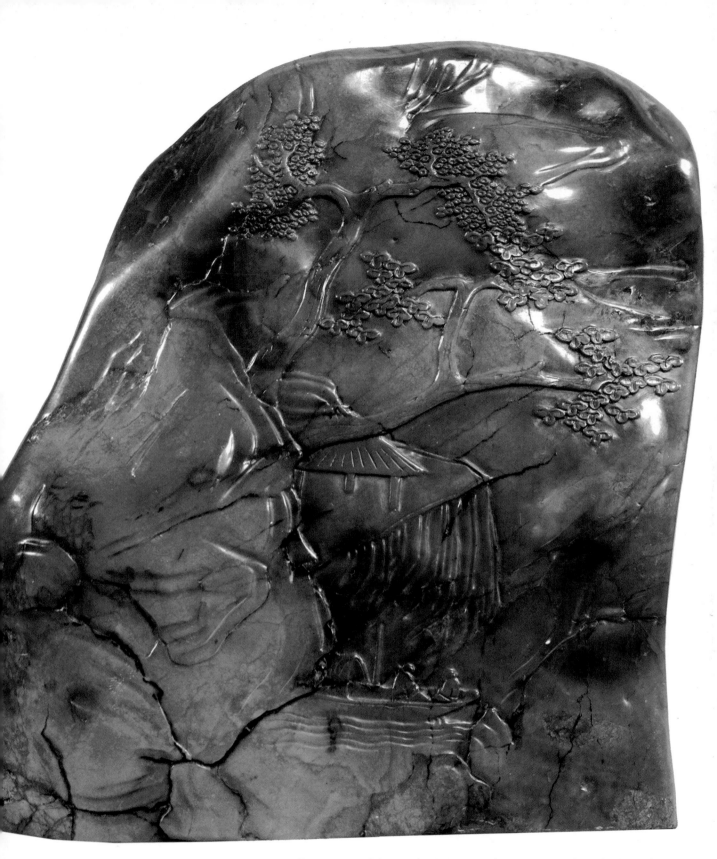

16 The garden of Daisen-in, Daitoku-ji, Kyoto, made in the early sixteenth century. The gravel representing water and the rocks representing mountains condense an image of nature—a Taoist-inspired landscape symbol often made in Zen monasteries

17 Illustration of the 'Red Cliff' poem by Su Tung-p'o. The 'veins' of the terrain are emphatically marked. A hermit's hut stands on the hillside and a pleasure-boat floats on the river with two people in the foreground. The Red Cliff is an escarpment overlooking the Yangtze near Huang-chou, which after the famous Sung poet-painter had written his prose poems in 1082 was to become a symbol of nature-consciousness and inspire many works of literature and art during the following centuries. Soapstone seal, sixteenth to seventeenth century, Ming dynasty, h. 7$\frac{1}{8}$ in.

首徙 不秋 谷慶 遊 方 眠 阻 但

一小斷絕 近問 往信 教想 為芳

未期歎 善 無以 炎光 極

況轉進復慕為

永轉蓋善堂亡 充実極

无緒人 乏此時 如何 以 下此時 如何 適 氣傷人 足下此時 如何 適

新喜當遠 遠 達 二別 草草

叙竟 想追尋 謹遣 一行 市乘

18 'Grass' script
calligraphy by an
unknown T'ang artist.
The style is very close
to the Taoist 'cloud'
script which expresses
the motions of Vital
Energy. T'ang dynasty

19 *Looking towards the
Waterfall* by Chang
Feng (fl. 1640–52), a
superb calligraphic
drawing of a landscape
in contrasting wet and
dry brush-technique.
Ink on paper $67\frac{3}{4} \times 24$ in.

20 Esoteric Taoist brushed calligraphic mark of the cloud script in crimson, meaning both *lung* (dragon) and *ch'ing* (blue), decorating a sacrificial Chün bowl. Twelfth century, Sung dynasty, d. $5\frac{3}{8}$ in.

21 Communist May Day rally in Peking, the floating ribbons with slogans suspended from the flying balloons conveying the magic power of the esoteric cloud script calligraphy

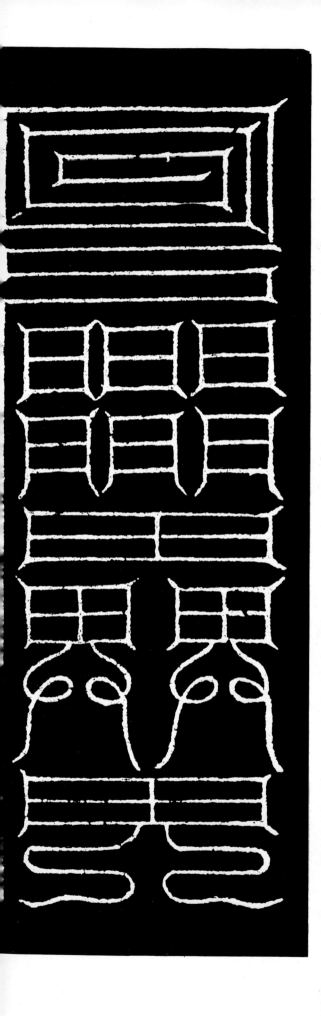
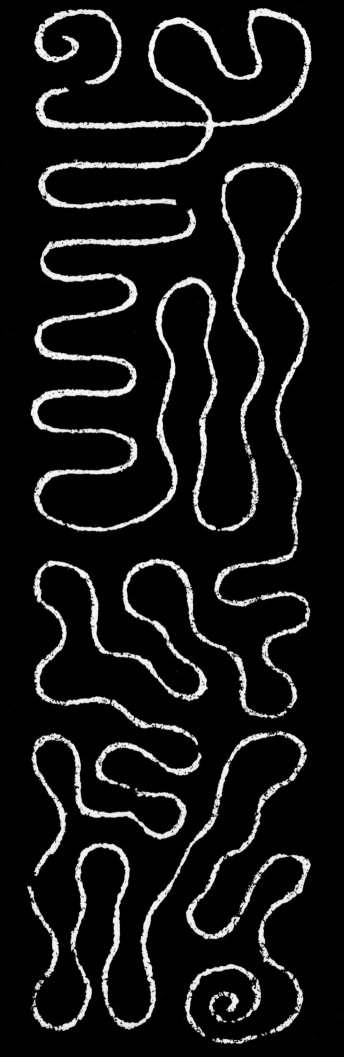

22 A magic diagram to
rid the eastern quarters of
a dwelling of evil
spirits, in a style of Taoist
calligraphy reflecting the
sharpness of the yang
element, and carpentry
technique. Eleventh
century, Sung dynasty.
Reproduced from the
Taoist Canon (*Tao-tsang*)

23 A magic diagram, one
of a set of nine, in a
rounded style of Taoist
calligraphy reflecting the
sinuous motion of the yin
element, and needlework
technique. Eleventh
century, Sung dynasty.
Reproduced from the
Taoist Canon (*Tao-tsang*)

24 Tortoise entwined with
a snake, symbolizing the
north, night, winter and
the abyss of yin. Stone
rubbing after Wu Tao-tzu,
the great Buddhist painter
of the T'ang dynasty

25 A shepherdess (yin) surrounded by three sheep (*yang*), a pun-symbol for yang meaning male. The whole design, with two male and one female sheep, symbolizes the trigram 'the Lake': ☱ . *Famille rose* egg-shell porcelain dish, Yung-cheng period (1723–35), Ch'ing dynasty, d. $7\frac{7}{8}$ in.

26 *Flowering Hills in the Height of Spring* by Lan Ying (1585–1664) of the Ming dynasty. The composition contains the Taoist geomantic 'dragon veins' which lend magic power to painting. Ink and colours on silk, $122\frac{1}{2} \times 40\frac{1}{8}$ in.

27 Plum blossom.
Calligraphic design of
the flower of winter,
symbol of sexual vitality.
Attributed to Wang
Mien (1335–1407) of the
Yüan dynasty. Stone
rubbing $43\frac{1}{4} \times 22$ in.

28 Liu-hai the Immortal,
a good luck charm partly
composed of calligraphic
elements in the style and
arrangement of Taoist
magic diagrams.
Nineteenth century,
Ch'ing dynasty, stone
rubbing $24\frac{3}{8} \times 8\frac{1}{4}$ in.

29 Flat jade vase of gourd shape symbolic of the union of yang and yin, Heaven and Earth, male and female. The Southern Sung tradition of the red (yin) and green (yang) sacrificial colour combination reinforces this symbolic harmony. The two-character *t'ai chi* 'Great Luck' inscription in red is also a pun symbol for *t'ai chi* meaning the Great Ultimate. Mid-eighteenth century, Ch'ing dynasty, h. 11 in.

30 The survival of popular Taoism reflected in a Maoist demonstration in Hopei Province in 1968. The huge portrait of Chairman Mao is flanked by double-*hsi*, 'double happiness' characters, a traditional Taoist sign for good augury. The red and green colour-scheme is also Taoist

31 Lao-tzu (also known as
Lao Chün or Lao Tan),
commonly regarded as the
originator of Taoism. He
holds a scroll in one hand
and is riding a water
buffalo on which, accord-
ing to legend, he left China
to travel towards the west.
Seventeenth century, Ming
dynasty, bronze h. 27½ in.

32 A Taoist hermit in
ragged garments, executed
in village craft style.
c. 1800, Ch'ing dynasty,
birch root h. 34⅝ in.

33 Rare and early carving of a Taoist deity with traces of red and blue and showing strong stylistic influence from Buddhist sculpture. Late tenth to early twelfth century, Northern Sung dynasty, wood h. $75\frac{5}{8}$ in.

34 The Northern Dipper (Constellation of the Great Bear). A procession of the gods of the Heavenly Constellations, detail from one of a pair of great Taoist frescoes. End of thirteenth to beginning of fourteenth century, Yüan dynasty. Originally in a temple near P'ing-yang area in South Shansi. Whole fresco 367 × 248 in.

35 Realm of the Immortals, with yin spirits carrying ceremonial lanterns, brooms and parasols descending on clouds from a misty valley to reach the domain of yang, symbolized by the phallic-shaped rock formation in the foreground. Detail from a handscroll, school of Li Kung-lin (1040–1106), Northern Sung dynasty

36 Realm of the Immortals. This detail from the same handscroll depicts yang spirits as a group of scholars in an open pavilion with a rock formation in the foreground. They are meeting the world of yin, symbolized by the solitary Immortal outside the pavilion and the deep misty valley beyond the edge of the precipice. These two scroll details illustrate the assimilation by Taoist adepts of yin and yang energies from the natural world

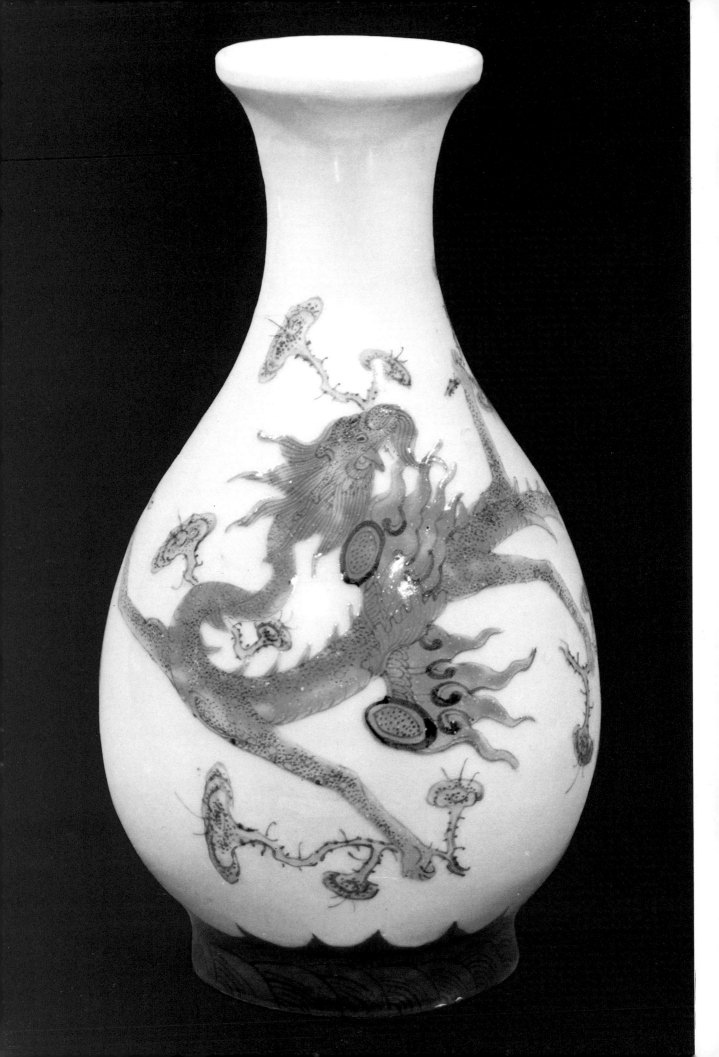

37 Vase decorated with a blue-winged dragon, representing Heaven and yang, carrying red ling-chih fungi, representing Earth and yin. Four-character Yung-cheng mark (1723–35) but *c*. 1800, h. 6½ in.

38 'The Leaping White Tiger' or 'The Attack from the Rear'. Sexual union of yang and yin, the penetration by the yang dragon of the yin vase. Album leaf in ink and colours on silk, K'ang-hsi period (1662–1722), Ch'ing dynasty

39 Sexual union on the water; yin-yang union at the common human level. Album leaf in ink and touches of colour, nineteenth century, Ch'ing dynasty

40 *Travellers Among Snowy Hills*, attributed to Li Ch'eng (*c.* 916–67) of the Northern Sung dynasty. Cloud-shaped mountains emphasize the yin-element which dominates winter. Ink and colour on silk

41 *Temple on a Clear Day in the Mountains*, also attributed to Li Ch'eng. Sharpness and clarity symbolize yang, the 'bright' element. Ink and colour on silk. In these two paintings the polar forces of yin and yang appear in their more esoteric form

42 *The 'Jade Lady' Among Clouds* (detail) by Ts'ui Tzu-chung. She is riding on a 'rising dragon vortex' cloud formation, filled with airy music. She personifies the esoteric yin which is combined for meditation with the male Taoist's personal yang. Ink and colour on silk $66\frac{1}{2} \times 20\frac{1}{2}$ in.

43 Two women in a garden are surrounded by female emblems—cloud, fungus, peonies etc. A male Feng-bird flies down to them. Cranes of immortality are in the border. An allegorical representation of domestic Taoism. *Famille rose* porcelain plate, late eighteenth century, d. $8\frac{1}{4}$ in.

44 *Mountain Landscape* (detail) by Huang Kung-wang, Yuan dynasty (1269–1354).
The style of this picture combines all the Chinese virtues of modesty, clarity and
simplicity, and illustrates the harmony which is the goal of all Taoist action and
non-action. Dragon veins run through the mountain massifs, yang vitalizing the
yin earth

46 Flowery symbols of yin decorating a dish. Their qualities would be transmitted to the food the dish was meant to contain, and so be absorbed by whoever ate it. *Famille rose* porcelain, mid-eighteenth century, d. 8¼ in.

45 *In the Garden on a Rocky Seat.* The tree is marked with constellation 'holes' shaped to represent the Taoist cloud script character for 'union' or 'harmony'. The open peony symbolizes the female genitals. Album leaf in ink and colours on silk. K'ang-hsi period (1662–1722), Ch'ing dynasty

47 Wooden stand with rocks (Earth), defined by negative shapes spotted with constellation 'holes' (Heaven). Eighteenth century, Ch'ing dynasty, d. 5⅛ in.

48 Landscape by Tao Chi (1641–1717). The emphatic roughness of the calligraphic time-lines in the rocks contrasts yang with the misty yin dots. Ch'ing dynasty. Album leaf in ink and colours on paper, 11 × 9½ in.

49 Two lovers interlocked, symbolizing the harmony of yin and yang, in the Taoist 'Hovering Butterflies' position, the eleventh of the *Thirty Heaven and Earth Postures*. In this position, 'Lord Yang lies on his back and faces upwards. Lady Yin seats herself on his stomach placing her feet firmly in the bedding. She then reaches behind for his Jade Root, then slides on to it with backward movement.' Porcelain, mid-eighteenth century, Ch'ing dynasty, h. $1\frac{7}{8}$ in.

50 The Taoist 'Autumn Days' posture, the last of the *Thirty Heaven and Earth Postures*. 'The Lord Yang lies on his back, his hand at the back of his head, and Lady Yin sits on his stomach but turning her face to his feet. As they have enjoyed twenty-nine positions without pause he contemplates, and, since he cannot see her face, imagines her to be the Great Yin Spirit herself. Her hands have also encouraged this illusion, and as the Jade Stem stiffens, she raises herself on to it.' *Famille verte* porcelain cup, K'ang-hsi period (1662–1722), Ch'ing dynasty, d. $2\frac{3}{4}$ in.

51 Domestic wall-hanging embroidered with the image of Hsi-wang-mu, the Queen Mother of the West, with phoenix and offering dish, and three bats (fu) pun symbol for happiness. The Eight Immortals appear at the sides. Late nineteenth century, Ch'ing dynasty, $110\frac{1}{4} \times 59$ in.

52 The character shou (long life) in 'grass' script calligraphy, composed to resemble the Taoist 'internal circulation' diagram (see plate 53). Signed by the eighty-five-year-old Yeh Chih with the seal of the artist. Rubbing dated first day of the first moon, 1863, Ch'ing dynasty, $44\frac{1}{8} \times 24\frac{3}{4}$ in.

53 Diagram of the 'subtle body' mapping the Inner Alchemy. Rubbing dated 1886, Ch'ing dynasty

54 The sacred Taoist script form of the character shou, 'long life', linking Heaven with Earth and guarded by dragons. The pattern reflects part of the inner meditative process. Painted lacquer brush-pot, Wan-li period (1573–1620), Ming dynasty, h. 13 in.

55 The Rising Celestial Dragon with the pearl representing condensed human-cosmic energy. Detail of a mandarin robe of embroidered silk, Chia-ch'ing period (1796–1820), Ch'ing dynasty

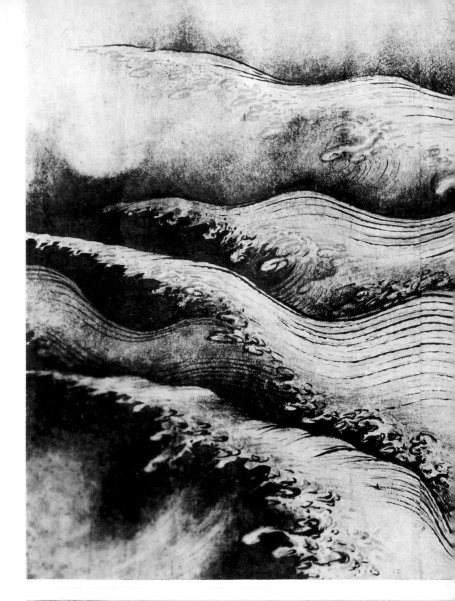

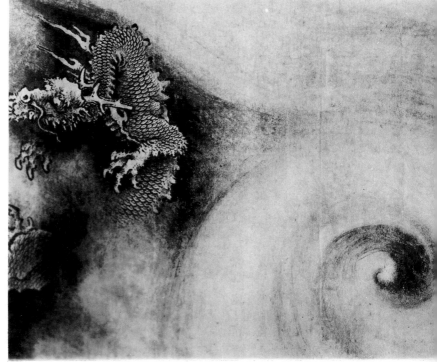

56, 57 Dragons among
vortices of cloud and water;
they refer to the forces at
once outer and inner which
are harnessed in the Inner
Alchemy, their horned and
whiskered heads representing yang, their scales yin.
Details of the Nine Dragon
Scroll by Ch'en Jung,
dated 1244, Sung dynasty,
ink and slight colour on
paper, h. 18⅛ in.

58 Immortals (hsien) in a celestial boat bound for the Taoist Island Paradise. Te-hua porcelain, early seventeenth century, Ming dynasty, h. 11¾ in.

59 Popular polychrome image of a Taoist Immortal offering the female peaches of longevity from a ju-i ('as you wish') sceptre-shaped open basket, symbol of the female sexual organ with its juices. Early nineteenth century, Ch'ing dynasty, porcelain h. 18½ in.

60 Dragon emblem of both Imperial power and inner energy, guarding the fiery concentration of yin-yang. Detail, *famille noir* vase, early eighteenth century, Ch'ing dynasty, h. 27½ in.

62 Shou-lao, star god of Longevity, holding a dragon-headed staff with a gourd containing the elixir of life attached to one hand, and the peach of eternal life with a crane inside in the other. Late eighteenth century, Ch'ing dynasty, soapstone h. 19¼ in.

61 *Pines and Cranes* by Chu Chi-i, dated 1740. Popular Taoist symbols of the long life that is to be gained by sexual and meditative practices. Rubbing 66⅞ × 32¼ in.

63 Taoists, the one in the red robe wearing the famous Taoist fragrant cap, the most important outward sign of the adept. Porcelain brush-pot decorated in *famille verte* enamels, K'ang-hsi period (1662–1722), Ch'ing dynasty, h. 5½ in.

64 Taoist children playing at schools on a terrace. They represent Taoist adepts reborn by their Inner Alchemy into the paradise of Immortality. Blue and white porcelain dish, Wan-li period (1573–1619), Ming dynasty, d. 11½ in.

65 Taoist deity in possession of yin symbols, such as a vessel, ju-i sceptre, coral etc. *c.* 1800, Ch'ing dynasty, carved ivory h. 10¼ in.

66 The winter-night-yin symbol of tortoise and snake entwined, combined with the attributes of dragon and tiger, symbolic of spring and autumn, thus suggesting the inner unification of the whole cycle. Japanese bronze, signed Seimu, early nineteenth century, h. 6¼ in.

67 *Among Green Mountains I build a House* by K'un-ts'an (*c.* 1610–93), an autumn painting dated the first day of the tenth month 1663. The style captures the culminating spirit of tranquillity in Tao attained by hermits. Ch'ing dynasty. Ink and colour on silk, 35 × 13¾ in.

DOCUMENTARY ILLUSTRATIONS
AND COMMENTARIES

As preface we give below a translation of the second prose poem (fu) written by Su Tung-p'o (1037–1101) on the Red Cliff, and with it one of the many works of art his poems inspired (see also *plate 17*). The symbolic significance (of fish, mountains, etc.) will be apparent to readers of the Introduction on the earlier pages of this book.

THE RED CLIFF

This year, on the fifteenth day of the tenth moon, I was walking back from Snow Hall to my home at Lin-kao. I had two guests with me, and we went along the bank of the Yellow Mud. Icy dew had already fallen and the trees were bare of leaves. Our shadows appeared on the ground, and looking up we saw the bright moon. Glancing around to enjoy the sight, we walked along singing in turns.

After a while, I sighed and said, 'Here I have guests and there is no wine! Even if I had some wine, there is no savoury food to eat with it. The moon is clear, the breeze is fresh, what shall we do with such a fine night?'

One of my guests said, 'Today towards sundown I put out a net and caught some fish with large mouths and small scales, like the perch of Pine River. Can we look round to find some wine?'

As soon as we got home I consulted my wife. She said, 'I have a gallon of wine. I have stored it for a long time waiting for an occasion when you might need it unexpectedly.' So we took the wine and fish and went for a trip to the foot of the Red Cliff. The river raced along noisily, its sheer banks rising to a thousand feet. The mountains were high, the moon was small. The water level had dropped, leaving boulders protruding. How many days or months had passed since my last visit? The river and the mountains, I could not recognize them again!

But holding up my robe, I began to climb, walking along precipitous slopes, opening up hidden growth of plants, crouching like tigers and leopards, ascending like curly dragons. I pulled my way up to perch at the precarious nest of the migratory falcon and looked down into the dark palace of the God of Rivers. My two guests could not follow me there. Shrilly, I gave a long cry. The grass and the trees swayed and shook, the mountains rang, and the valleys echoed. The wind came up and the water bubbled, and I felt a gentle chill of sadness. Shivering with cold, I knew that I could not stay there any longer.

I went back to my guests and got into the boat and turned it loose in mid-stream, content to rest wherever it stopped. The night was almost half over and all around was silent and still. Suddenly a lonely crane appeared, cutting across the river from the east. Its wings were like cart-wheels, and it wore a black robe and a coat of white silk. With a long, strange cry, it swooped over my boat and went off to the west.

Soon afterwards my guests left and I, too, promptly went to sleep. I dreamed I saw a Taoist priest in a feather robe fluttering as an Immortal, down the road past the foot of Lin-kao. He bowed to me and said, 'Did you enjoy your outing to the Red Cliff?' I asked him his name, but he looked down and did not answer. 'Ah! Dear me! I know you! Last night, something passed me, flying over and crying; that was you, was it not?'

The Taoist priest turned his head round to look and laughed. Then I woke up with a start. I opened the door to have a look at him, but there was no sign of him.

1 Illustration to Su Tung-p'o's poem 'The Red Cliff'. Detail of handscroll attributed to Chu Jui, fl. early 12th century, Sung dynasty. National Palace collection, Taipei, Taiwan, Republic of China.

2 Carved wood stand representing rock formations, late 17th century, Ch'ing dynasty. h. $2\frac{3}{8}$ in. Gulbenkian Museum, Durham.

I The natural world

The observation of nature through the eyes of the Taoist hermits evolved the art of active participation in the discovery of the mysterious forces of nature (e.g. 'dragon veins'), frequently by viewing things produced by nature and/or man on a miniature scale (e.g. rock-gardens). These provided a setting for mystical explorations, spiritual journeys: thus landscapes were not only to have material existence, but also to reach out into the Realm of the Immortals and Spirits.

3

4

5

6

7

9

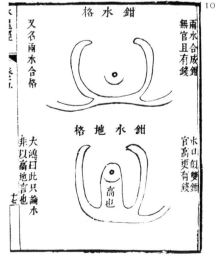

10

3 *A Quiet Life in a Wooded Glen,* by Wang Meng, *c.* 1308–85. A hermit's hut enclosed by a vase-shaped tree-formation. Ink and colour on paper, 5ft. 10 in. × 25¼ in. Courtesy of the Art Institute of Chicago.

4 T'ai-hu stone in a devastated garden in Soochow, photographed in the 1930s.

5 Turquoise matrix-mountain with hermit's hut, pines, deer and waterfall, 18th century, Ch'ing dynasty, h. 9 in. British Museum.

6 Garden with T'ai-hu stone formation. Early 17th-century block-print. From *Ku-pen Hsi-ch'ü Ts'ung-k'an.*

7 'Dragon vein' markings and calligraphic designs on a soapstone pebble seal. 18th century, Ch'ing dynasty, h. 3⅛ in. Gulbenkian Museum, Durham.

8 Landscape with pronounced 'dragon veins' by Huang Kungwang, Yüan dynasty (1269–1354). Detail. National Palace collection, Taiwan.

9 Landscape by Fan Yün, dated 1696–7. Ink and colour on silk, 69⅝ × 22¼ in. Gulbenkian Museum, Durham.

10 'Dragon veins' and vital locations for yin and yang in sexological terms, expressed in relevant anatomical details of the human body. An illustration from the 1744–5 edition of the *Shui-lung ching,* a geomancy classic.

11 Japanese porcelain tea-pot imitating wood-carving and symbolizing wood. Mid-18th century, h. 6½ in. Private collection.
12 Carved wood stand with fungus, constellation holes and bosses, 17th–18th century, Ch'ing dynasty, l. 6¾ in. Gulbenkian Museum, Durham.
13 Waves and water-plants on a Celadon bowl of the 12th century, Sung dynasty, d. 5¼ in. Barlow Collection, University of Sussex.

11

14

12

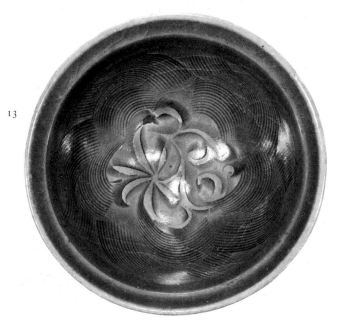

13

15

14 The Lion Grove in Soochow with artificial pond and 'mountains'.

15 Garden scene with yin dwarf-tree of cloud script calligraphy-shape in pot of crackled glaze (cold and winter), and yang miniature rock garden in tripod vessel (warm and summer), symbolizing a pair of lovers. Early 17th-century block-print.

16 Celadon vase with bamboo receptacle (yin) surrounded by banana leaves (yang). 18th century, Ch'ing dynasty, h. 9½ in. Victoria and Albert Museum, London.

17 Wine vessel with quails, symbols of affectionate love. 18th century, Ch'ing dynasty, h. 6½ in. Victoria and Albert Museum, London.

18 Peach-shaped box, carved red and black laquer with two dragons, *ch'un* (spring) character enclosing Shou-lao, god of Longevity; below, a bowl of lucky emblems. Border of peach (long life) and floral designs. A birthday present, Ch'ien-lung period (1736–96), Ch'ing dynasty, d. 14⅝ in. Gulbenkian Museum, Durham.

16

18

17

19

19 Three children under plum blossom, representing sexual pleasure, holding Taoist emblems, a ju-i sceptre and peaches. Detail. Ink and slight colours on silk, attributed to Liang K'ai (fl. 1250), but 16th century copy, Ming dynasty. Gulbenkian Museum, Durham.

II The moving spirit

Ch'i, the Moving, Cosmic Spirit vitalizes and infuses all things, for no distinction is made between the animate and the inanimate. It gives life to nature, growth to trees, movement to water, energy to man, and is exhaled by the mountains where the Immortals live as clouds and mist—hence the mystic power of landscapes. The Moving Spirit ('air', 'breath', 'vapour') is also in the centre of the very important Taoist breathing exercises which involve the art of smelling, and the use of incense.

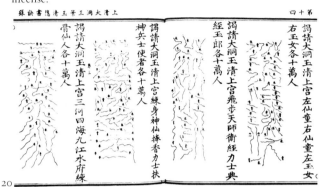

20

23

21

24

22

20 Diagrams showing ch'i (Vital Energy, air, etc.) patterns (also known as marble patterns) from a Sung work in the Taoist Canon (*Tao-tsang*).

21 Marbled design on a Japanese agate-ware tea-pot. This type of tea-pot with short spout and handle is usually associated with the 'nose-drinking' practised by southern Chinese during the 12th century—surely Taoists. The vessel was intended to aid the performance of certain breathing exercises by inhalation, mistakenly identified by uninitiated contemporary observers as 'drinking through the nose'. Ise Banko mark, early 19th century, h. 3 in. Private collection.

22 Imitation marbled-ware stem-bowl, glaze with feathered pattern, 16th–17th century, Ming dynasty, d. $5\frac{7}{8}$ in. Gulbenkian Museum, Durham.

23 Marbled bowl with wood-grain and feather pattern of Vital Energy, 13th century, Sung dynasty, d. $7\frac{3}{4}$ in. Victoria and Albert Museum, London.

24 Marbled ware vase, probably Sung dynasty, h. $7\frac{3}{4}$ in. Royal Scottish Museum, Edinburgh.

25 Phosphorus olive glaze with blue–white splashes to simulate blurred vision of rocks. Stoneware dish, 8th–9th century, T'ang dynasty, d. 11 in. British Museum.

26 Carved wood stand with Vital Energy design, 17th–18th century, Ch'ing dynasty, l. 5½ in. Gulbenkian Museum, Durham.

27 *Cloudy Mountains* by Mi Yu-jen, dated 1130, Southern Sung dynasty, ink and colour on silk, 17⅛ × 76½ in. Cleveland Museum of Art, Ohio, purchased from the J. H. Wade Fund.

28 *Misty Landscape*, attrib. Zen painter Ying Yü-chien, 12th–13th century. Detail handscroll. Tokugawa Museum, Nagoya.

25

26

27

28

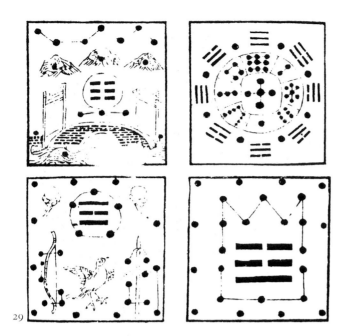

29

30

III Cycles of change

The Great Ultimate produces the positive-negative dualism of
yang and yin, and their continuous interaction in turn gives
birth to the five elements from which all events and objects are
derived. Trigrams and hexagrams are the most ancient emblems
of change, but directional, seasonal and colour symbols are also
constant reminders of it in Taoist visual art.

29 Cosmic diagrams from the Taoist Canon (*Tao-tsang*).

30 The interlocking yin-yang in the centre of a blue and white
porcelain dish represents the Great Ultimate (t'ai chi) and is
surrounded by eight trigrams (pa-kua). Ch'ien-lung period
(1736–96), Ch'ing dynasty, d. 6 in. Gulbenkian Museum,
Durham

31 Symbol of the Great Ultimate and trigrams on an octagonal
incense burner. Early nineteenth century, Ch'ing dynasty.
Brass, h. $4\frac{3}{8}$ in. Abbot Hall Art Gallery, Kendal.

32 Cosmic mirror decorated with the four directional animals,
the twelve zodiacs, twenty-eight constellations and a Taoist
inscription, 2nd-3rd century AD. Bronze, d. $7\frac{1}{2}$ in. Victoria and
Albert Museum, London.

33 Symbol of the Great Ultimate and trigrams on an octagonal
ink-cake. Made by Ch'eng Chung-fang in 1621, d. $4\frac{3}{4}$ in. Private
collection.

34 Yin-yang coin, decorated with King Wen's circular arrangement of the trigrams, called the Sequence of Later Heaven or
Inner World Arrangement. 18th century, Ch'ing dynasty,
d. $1\frac{5}{8}$ in. Gulbenkian Museum, Durham.

35 Jade amulet with symbol of the Great Ultimate and the
Twelve Earthly Branches guarded by dragon and phoenix, 16th
century, Ming dynasty, l. $2\frac{5}{8}$ in. Gulbenkian Museum, Durham.

36 Trigrams around the sides of a Celadon vessel, leaving the
opening, i.e. the receptacle, to represent the Great Ultimate,
12th-13th century, Sung dynasty, d. $6\frac{1}{4}$ in. Royal Scottish
Museum, Edinburgh.

37 *Winter Landscape* (detail) by Kuo Hsi, *c.* 1020–90, Sung
dynasty, ink on silk $21\frac{5}{8}$ in. × 15 ft. $9\frac{1}{4}$ in. The Toledo Museum
of Art, Ohio.

31

32

33

34

35

36

37

38

39

40

41

38–41 Spring, Summer, Autumn and Winter, from a set of eight seasonal album leaves attributed to Kung Hsien (fl. 1656–82) of the Ch'ing dynasty, ink and slight colour on paper $10\frac{5}{8} \times 11\frac{3}{8}$ in. Gulbenkian Museum, Durham.

IV Heaven and Earth

The unity of Heaven (yang) and Earth (yin) is the source of cosmic power and is symbolized by shapes, for example, the square (tsung) and the circle (pi) or in mirror designs or the double gourd or calabash, or by two-colour combinations, for instance black or blue or green for Heaven and crimson, purple or red for Earth. Constellation patterns (Heaven) dominate certain ceramic shapes representing Earth, or appear in calligraphic designs of earthly objects, frequently in an abstract fashion.

Man completes this unity, and we are frequently reminded of the threefold state of the universe.

42 Jade cosmic pi disc representing Heaven with a jade tsung representing Earth. Disc late Chou period, d. $5\frac{1}{4}$ in.; tsung Middle Chou period, h. $4\frac{3}{8}$ in. Gulbenkian Museum, Durham.
43 Cosmic mirror combining pi and tsung, Han period, bronze, d. $5\frac{1}{2}$ in. Barlow collection, University of Sussex.
44 Ceremonial sceptre with trigrams on the pi disc representing Heaven, wave and rocks on the shaft representing Earth. 15th-16th century, Ming dynasty, l. $18\frac{7}{8}$ in. Gulbenkian Museum, Durham.

42

43

44

45

47

48

46

45 Lovers symbolizing the harmony between Heaven and Earth through the union of yin and yang, 19th-century album painting. Roger Peyrefitte Collection, Paris.

46 Gourd-shaped vase symbolizing the unity of Heaven and Earth, decorated with calligraphic variations of the shou (long life) symbol. Early 17th century, Ming dynasty, h. 15 in. Victoria and Albert Museum.

47, 48 Jade jardiniere and its wooden stand symbolizing the unity of Heaven (clouds) and Earth (the waves of the stand). Imperial poetic inscription dated 1769, Ch'ing dynasty, l. 15¼ in. and 14 in. Gulbenkian Museum, Durham.

49 Clouds and constellations in a Taoist script related to the cloud script. From a 12th-century work in the Taoist Canon.

50 Stylized 'constellation' calligraphy from the stone engraving of a Han tomb.

51 Mottled glass cup with constellation dots in an abstract calligraphic style, 18th century, Ch'ing dynasty, h. 1¾ in. Gulbenkian Museum, Durham.

52 The spread of Vital Energy interpreted by stars and clouds in an abstract calligraphic style. From a 19th-century Taoist weather-manual. Ink on paper 9½ × 6¼ in. University Library, Durham.

53 Limestone incense vessel with tripod shape—an esoteric symbol of the male sex organ. The natural texture of the stone suggests constellations (Heaven) and dragon veins (Earth). 12th-13th century, Sung dynasty, d. 5⅛ in. Gulbenkian Museum, Durham.

54 Inlaid gold 'sun-spots' representing constellations on a bronze incense-burner. Four-character Hsüan-te seal-mark (1426–35), but mid-18th century, Ch'ing dynasty, h. 2½ in. Gulbenkian Museum, Durham.

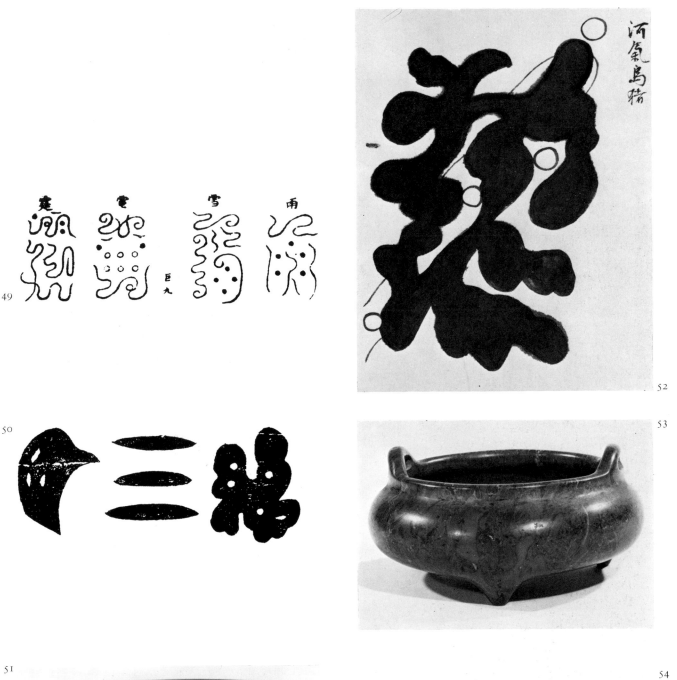

49

50

51

53

54

55

55 Heavenly dragon with constellation dots among earthly yin ling-chih fungi. Detail of gilt design on mirror-black vase. K'ang-hsi period (1662–1722), Ch'ing dynasty. Private collection.

56 Map of the sacred mountain known as the 'Mountain of Heavenly Kingdom', drawn in the esoteric calligraphic style of the constellation script. From the Taoist Canon.

57 Carved wood stand with naturalistic twisted root formations (Earth) and abstract constellation-type holes (Heaven), providing at least two different esoteric diagrams for the sacred location of spirits. Sung style, l. 9⅞ in. Gulbenkian Museum, Durham.

56

57

58 Three-sectioned pocket-size offering dishes for Taoist sacrifices. The lid has a clockwise spiral for yang (male). 12th century, Sung dynasty, d. 7⅛ in. Barlow collection, University of Sussex.

59 *Man desired by Three Sisters*. Album leaf painted in colours, 19th century. Roger Peyrefitte Collection, Paris.

60 Wooden tripod stand with three-fold Unity of Heaven, Earth and Mankind design. 18th-century style, Ch'ing dynasty, d. 4½ in. Gulbenkian Museum, Durham.

61 Three-fold vase of double-gourd shape. Porcelain, covered with an even tea-dust glaze. Yung-cheng period (1723–35), Ch'ing dynasty, h. 9½ in. Private collection.

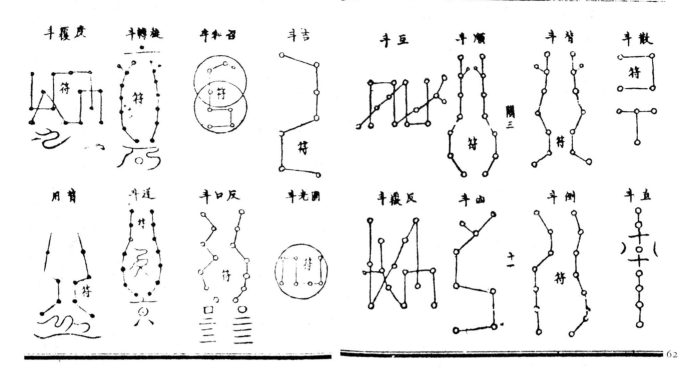

62

V Ritual

Sacrifices were the established Taoist form of public worship, which involved slaughtering sacrificial animals (pigs, chickens and fish) and displaying them with rice and wines on incense tables along with scriptures. Of all the sacrifices, the most important was the sacrifice offered to Heaven and Earth, and those to the deities of mountains, seas, and rivers. The private ritual of sexual intercourse played a significant part.

63

62 'Sculptural' shapes of ritual significance; earthly objects outlined by the stars of the constellations, some depicting the union of yin and yang in postures of sexual intercourse. From a 12th-century Sung work in the Taoist Canon.
63 Worship of the yang element with the aid of a dildo. Album painting in colour, 18th century. Ch'ing dynasty. Roger Peyrefitte Collection, Paris.
64 Worship of the yang element represented by a tripod vessel, emblem of the male sex organ. Early 17th century block print. National Library, Peking.
65 Tomb figure, Ch'ang-sha type, 4th-3rd century BC. Late Chou period, wood h. 9½ in. Private collection.
66 Supernatural creature with monster-head. Such hybrids were supposed to guard the entrances to K'un-lun, palace of the Lord of the Sky, or were tomb guardians. 7th-8th century, T'ang dynasty, pottery h. 11¾ in. Private collection.
67 Ritual of the union of yin and yang. Album painting in colour, 19th century. Roger Peyrefitte Collection, Paris.
68 Phallic-shaped guardian figure representing the Hare of the Chinese zodiac, late 6th century, Sui period, stone, h. 9½ in. Gulbenkian Museum, Durham.

64

65

66

67

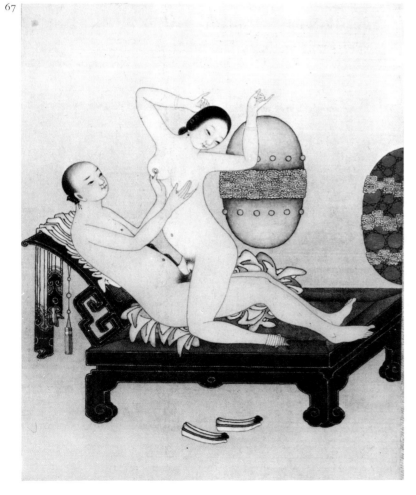

68

69, 70 Taoist priest's robe embroidered with cosmic emblems and symbols of the pantheon of popular Taoism, including the Eight Immortals on the sleeves. On the front, clouds (yin)

cranes and a pair of male kylins (yang). The two large characters on the back mean 'by imperial appointment'. *c.* 1800, Ch'ing dynasty. Private collection.

71 Construction of an altar. Detail of early 17th-century block-print.
72 Sacrificial display without the use of an altar, illustrating the popular drama *Records of the Thorn Hairpin* (records of the very poor). 15th-century block-print. National Library, Peking.

73

74

VI The mystical power of calligraphy

The world of Taoist calligraphy was always full of magic. Occult practices, some connected with sacrifices, used calligraphy and drawings for the sake of their magical power. Both calligraphy, including cipher and decorative script forms used for esoteric purposes, and painting were Taoist vehicles for the expression of the Vital Spirit (ch'i); hence their exceptional power, spiritual as well as artistic.

73 Taoists holding up sacred diagrams, detail from a wu-ts'ai porcelain saucer. Wan-li period (1573–1619), Ming dynasty, d. 5$\frac{1}{8}$ in. Private collection.
74 Consultation of a diagram. Early 17th century block-print.
75, 76 Taoist cloud script characters, 12th century, Taoist Canon, and example of the use of Taoist cloud script, from the Yüan edition of *The Western Chamber (Hsi-hsiang chi)*. National Library, Peking.
77 Cranes of longevity, their wings forming a 'feather forest'. Blue and white porcelain, probably Cheng-te period (1506–21); Ming dynasty, h. 15 in. Royal Scottish Museum, Edinburgh.
78 Diagram of the 'feather forest' from the Taoist Canon; based on the constellation of 45 stars, it was to bring about peace in the Empire.

77

75   76

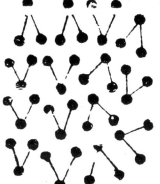

78

79

80

79, 80 A waterfall depicted with Taoist musical notes, from *The Sleeping Dragon Mountain*, attrib. to Li Kung-lin (1040–1106), and songs from the Taoist Canon.

81, 82 Ancient good luck design frequently employed in lattice-work, from the Taoist Canon, and lattice-work on the throne of Emperor K'ang-hsi (1662–1722) with good luck diagrams. Victoria and Albert Museum, London.

82

81

83 Magic script of the character shou (longevity), peaches and fungi. Tou-ts'ai porcelain saucer, Yung-cheng period (1723–35), Ch'ing dynasty, d. 4⅝ in. Gulbenkian Museum, Durham.
84 Magic diagrams composed of shou, hsi (happiness) and chi (good luck) characters. Porcelain cup and lid, mid-19th century, h. 3⅞ in. Bowes Museum, Barnard Castle, Co. Durham.
85 Example of mystic bird script. From *Cho-keng-lu* (1936 edn.).

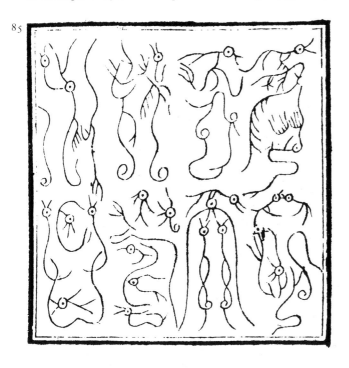

86 Tea-pot in the shape of the magic calligraphic form of shou (longevity), K'ang-hsi period (1662–1722), Ch'ing dynasty, h. 12⅝ in. Victoria and Albert Museum, London.

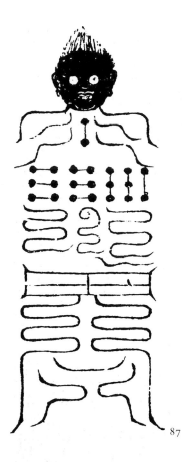

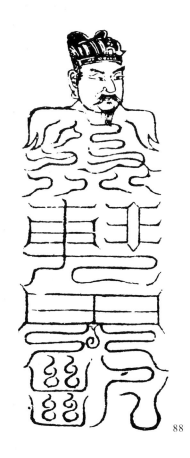

87

88

89

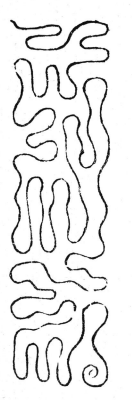

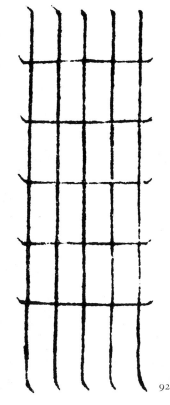

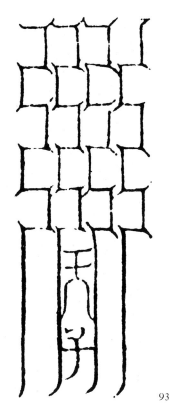

91

92

93

90

94

87–90 Masters of the Four Directions, north, west, south and east, a 13th-century talisman to nullify the effects of cursing. From the Taoist Canon.

91–3 Good luck charms from the Taoist Canon.

94 Sung dynasty charm composed of several esoteric script-forms. From the Taoist Canon.

95 Diagram for warding off fire, dated 1882, with a note: 'The Black Warrior's Diagram for warding off fire possesses the property of repelling unpropitious winds and extinguishing fires and has on numerous occasions shown its miraculous power. The Province of Chekiang suffers greatly from fire: this may be avoided by hanging up a copy of this Diagram (in your home). I, Te Hsing, Prefect of Chekiang from the Mountain of Eternal Snow (in Manchuria) selected 9 pm on the 6th day of the 3rd moon of the 8th year of Kuang-hsü (AD 1882); the Year Star then being in Yüan-i, the Heavenly Stem being Wu, the sign of the month being Pi, the Sun on its orbit having attained its nadir, the Moon being in its constellation of Ching (Well), Saturn (Earth) in that of Lou, Jupiter (Wood) in that of Mao, Mars (Fire) in that of Ching (Well), Venus (Metal) in that of Wei, and Mercury (Water) in that of Kuei; as being an auspicious period in which to copy the Diagram. I accordingly instructed [. . .] to superintend the engraving of it in stone to be set up in the four corners of the cities of the Province, to dispel the malignant geomantic influences and enable the people to procure rubbings.' Rubbing $40\frac{1}{2} \times 20\frac{1}{2}$ in. Private collection.

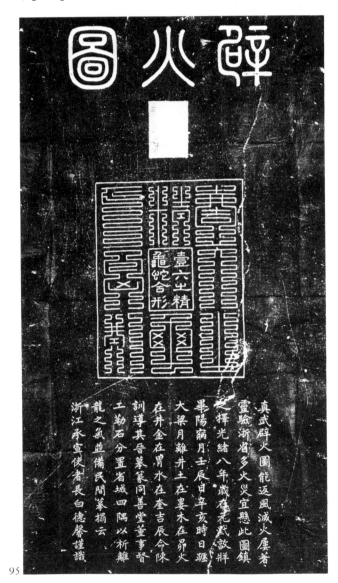

95

96

97

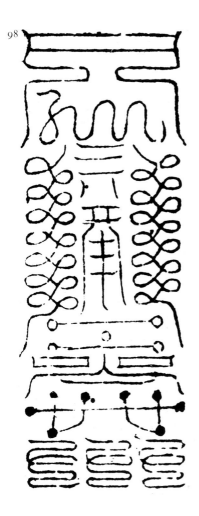

98

96 Magic diagram to raise wind, from the Taoist Canon.
97 *Diagram of Change* inlaid in gold on a bronze vase, 12th-13th century, Sung dynasty, h. 5⅛ in. Royal Scottish Museum, Edinburgh.
98 *Diagram of Change* using the elements of the ancient monster-mask. From a Sung work in the Taoist Canon.

VII Secret practices

The visual representations of Taoist alchemy and medical ideas covered a very wide field, from sketchy circulation diagrams to realistically modelled vagina-shaped medicinal cups. The former gave compositional inspiration for painters as symbols for the preservation of Vital Energy which, in this context, meant sexual energy. The cups symbolized the healing power of the female sex organ for man, evoking the cosmic force of the union of yin and yang. Sick or ailing men were to be cured by the secretion of yin essence from the cup, i.e. the symbolic vagina, as if the secretion was the result of an actual sexual intercourse charged with cosmic energy. A remarkable range of aphrodisiac instruments and exercises, such as the art of *t'ai-chi-chuan* evolved from this principle. Astrology, palmistry, physiognomy and geomancy were also among the main branches of occult arts.

99 Landscape ('split pagoda') interpretation of the Internal Circulation, at the centre of a Swatow dish, early 17th century, Ming dynasty, d. 16¼ in. Gulbenkian Museum, Durham.
100 Preliminary caresses on a bed decorated with crackled panels which symbolize the rising energy of the male which vitalizes the brain. Album painting, 19th century, Ch'ing dynasty. Roger Peyrefitte Collection, Paris.
101 Charm to vitalize the brain, composed of crackled calligraphic pattern, Sung period. From the Taoist Canon.

99

101

100

102

103

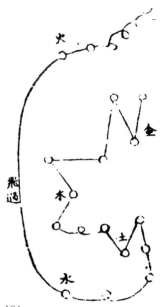

104

105

106

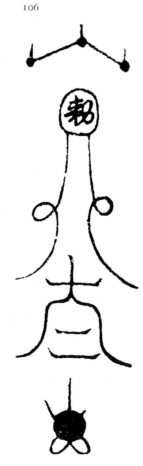

107

102 *T'ai-chi-chuan* shadow-boxing exercises in a Peking park, 1966.
103 Bronze perfumer still, 10th–12th century, Sung dynasty, British Museum.
104 The interdependence of the Five Elements interpreted in terms of the Internal Circulation. Sung work on divination and conjuration in the Taoist Canon.
105 Jade seal of phallic shape with dragon-among-cloud design, 18th century, Ch'ing dynasty, h. 4 in. Gulbenkian Museum, Durham.
106 Phallus-shaped diagram of the Heavenly Cure recommended for women. From the Taoist Canon.
107 Woman arousing her sleeping lover in a garden pavilion. Album painting, 18th century, Ch'ing dynasty. Roger Peyrefitte Collection, Paris.

108 *Misty Landscape*, attrib. Mi Fei, 1051–1107, Northern Sung dynasty. Yin mist is painted 'in reverse' in the wavy lines of hills shaped like vulva. Ink on silk, 59 × 30¾ in. Freer Gallery of Art, Washington.
109 Vagina-shaped rhino-horn medicinal cup, 16th century, Ming dynasty, h. 2½ in. Private collection.
110 Medicinal cup of rhino-horn, decorated with yin essence, carved inside with a figure of the T'ang hermit-poet, Chang Ch'ien (fl. *c.* 727), symbolically drifting down the Yangtze in his pleasure-boat of a hollow tree. Early 17th century, Ming dynasty, h. 3⅞ in. Private collection.
111 Rhino-horn cup with cloud design and dragon inside, 18th century, Ch'ing dynasty, h. 2½ in. Gulbenkian Museum, Durham.

109

110

111

108

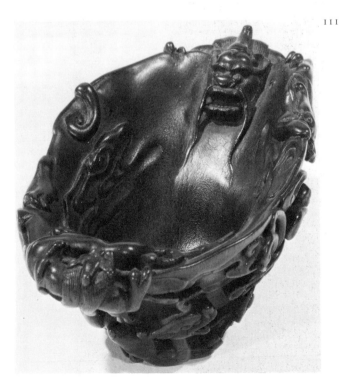

112

113

114

112 Eight-sided carved black (Heaven) lacquer box with cloud design. 13th century, Sung dynasty, d. $9\frac{7}{8}$ in. Royal Scottish Museum, Edinburgh.

113 Immortals in a rustic carved boat bound for the Taoist Paradise. From the yin vase flies cloud and five bats (fu), pun symbols for five-fold happiness (fu). After Ch'iu Ying (c. 1500–1550) by 'Lang Shih-ning', the Italian Jesuit painter Giuseppe Castiglione (1688–1768) at the court of the 18th century emperors K'ang-hsi, Yung-cheng and Ch'ien-lung. Detail of handscroll, ink and colours on silk. Private collection.

114 Immortal with vase (yin), from which emerges a cloud-fungus, emblematic of the female effluvia. At her feet is a male kylin. 17th century, Ming dynasty, hardstone, h. $2\frac{1}{2}$ in. Gulbenkian Museum, Durham.

VIII The Realm of the Immortals

While in terms of abstract ideas landscapes were to reach out into the realm of the Spirits, the Taoist popular art was primarily concerned with representational forms of the Immortals with combined symbolic attributes. The output of this art was enormous, ranging from ivory and porcelain figures to primitive painted paper images of domestic gods.

115 *The Supreme Taoist Master holding court* (detail) by Liang K'ai (fl. 1250). Ink on paper. H. C. Weng collection, New York.
116 The Great King of All the Dragons. Detail of handscroll, *The Metamorphoses of Heavenly Beings*, 11th century, Northern Sung dynasty, British Museum.

115

116

117

117 Hsi-wang-mu, Queen Mother of the West, riding a deer with fungus and peach, all symbols of longevity. Late 17th century, Ch'ing dynasty, soapstone, h. 9½ in. Gulbenkian Museum, Durham.

118 The Taoist Paradise. Detail of screen. Early 17th century, Ming dynasty, whole screen 26 ft. 3 in. × 13 ft. 1½ in. Gulbenkian Museum, Durham.

119 Chiang Tzu-ya in a priest's robe and hat, and carrying a yang 'audience tablet' with the name of Wu Wang, founder of the Chou dynasty. Behind him a spirit, Po Chien, holds a pennant used for summoning spirits. Early 17th century, Ming dynasty, ivory, h. 16⅛ in. Sassoon collection.

120 Lao-tzu with Taoist fragrant cap, in which the pearl symbolizes the accumulated Vital Energy, holding a scroll with interlocking yin-yang symbol and a whisk. By his side is a sheep with the fungus of immortality. Late 17th century, Ch'ing dynasty, ivory, h. 23¼ in. Sassoon collection.

121 Liu-hai, the Immortal, by Yen Hui, 14th century. Ink and colour on silk 66⅛ × 30¾ in. Chion-ji, Japan.

122 Li T'ieh-kuai, the Immortal, by the same artist. 63 × 30¾ in. Chion-ji, Japan.

123 *Two Immortals* by Wu Wei (1458–1508). Ink on paper, 27⅛ × 15⅜ in. National Palace collection, Taiwan.

124 Liu-hai the Immortal with the three-legged yin toad. Mid-18th century, Ch'ing dynasty, blue and white porcelain, h. 10¼ in. Gulbenkian Museum, Durham.

125 Li Tieh-kuai the Immortal, 19th century, Ch'ing dynasty, porcelain h. 13¾ in. Bowes Museum, Barnard Castle, Co. Durham.

126 One of the Eight Immortals, red cartouché from a crackled green glaze Celadon vase, 13th-14th century, Yüan dynasty, whole vase h. 13⅜ in. British Museum.

118

119

120

121

122

123

124

125

126

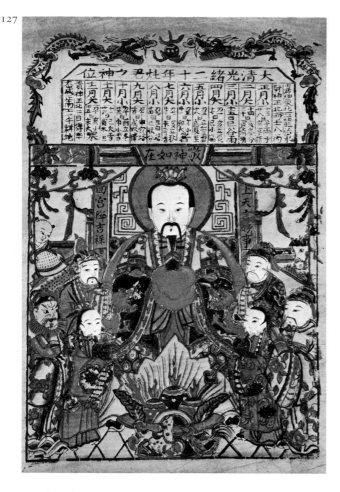

127 The Kitchen God from the large pantheon of popular Taoism. Dated 1895, Ch'ing dynasty. Ink and colours on paper, $13\frac{3}{8} \times 9\frac{1}{4}$ in. Gulbenkian Museum, Durham.
128 Demon, carved birch-wood. 19th century, Ch'ing dynasty, h. $7\frac{1}{4}$ in. Hancock Museum, Newcastle-upon-Tyne.
129 Immortal with a crane holding ling-chih fungus, 18th century, Ch'ing dynasty, h. 3 in. Gulbenkian Museum, Durham.